Penguin Handbooks
Cooking with Wine

Robin McDouall was born in Camberley in
1908 and educated at Haileybury and Trinity
College, Oxford. He started work in the
Gordon Hotels and worked in the kitchen of the
May Fair Hotel under Monsieur Berthaud,
where he learnt the foundations of classical
French cookery. For the five years before the
Second World War he was secretary to
Christopher Turnor, which involved a good
deal of travel and cookery. During the war he
was a navigator in the R.A.F. He was 'released'
as a Wing Commander in 1945, and took up
his present position as secretary to the
'Travellers' Club, where he is also in charge
of the catering.

Robin McDouall is the travel editor of the
Glasgow Herald and the cookery writer for
Fashion. He has contributed to *The Times*, the
Spectator, *The Times Literary Supplement*, *Vogue*,
Harper's Bazaar, *Wine & Food*, and other papers.

Cooking
with Wine

ROBIN McDOUALL

Illustrated by John Tribe

PENGUIN BOOKS

Penguin Books Ltd, Harmondsworth,
Middlesex, England
Penguin Books Inc., 7110 Ambassador Road,
Baltimore, Maryland 21207, U.S.A.
Penguin Books Australia Ltd, Ringwood,
Victoria, Australia
Penguin Books Canada Ltd,
41 Steelcase Road West,
Markham, Ontario, Canada

First published by Allen Lane The Penguin Press 1968
Published in Penguin Handbooks 1969
Reprinted 1971, 1973, 1974
Copyright © Robin McDouall, 1968

Made and printed in Great Britain by
Cox & Wyman Ltd, London, Reading and Fakenham
Set in Monotype Bembo

Title-page decoration by Quentin Blake

Contents

Introduction

Before one has started a book, before it is on the market, before one knows if anyone is going to buy it, it is, perhaps, both absurd and presumptuous to think of writing a sequel. Nevertheless, the thought comes into my head that there should be a companion volume to this, called *Cooking without Wine*. It would be longer, for there are more recipes that do not call for wine than recipes which do. Taking the title *Cooking with Wine* has, in fact, been an arbitrary decision to choose certain recipes, not necessarily the best, but merely a collection in which wine is an essential ingredient.

One could write a book called *Cooking with Eggs* or, more difficult, a book called *Cooking without Eggs*; a book called *Cooking with Butter* or, much more difficult, *Cooking without Butter*. I have written about cooking with wine because there are some people who think that there is something mysterious about cooking with wine, something un-English, something exotic, strange and what the Frogs do. I have tried to show, in a series of mainly simple recipes, that there is nothing odder about using wine as an ingredient than butter, eggs, flour or, getting rather more way-out, garlic or tarragon.

Cooking with Wine is an inexact title, as I have included beer, cyder and spirits. *Cooking with Alcohol* might have been more exact, but it suggests cooking on a spirit lamp – a spirit lamp filled with drinkable or chemical spirits, rather than methylated. I thought of *Booze in the Kitchen* but that conjured up the not altogether untrue picture of the cook with saucepan in one hand and a glass of gin in the other. (Cooking makes one so thirsty, my dear.) I thought of calling it *Bacchus in the Kitchen* in humble imitation of Norman Douglas' *Venus in the Kitchen* – he taught me, among other things, how to make an index and a sauce for cold asparagus. Anyway, here it is, and I hope it will prove to the timid cook that there is nothing stranger or more difficult in using wine in recipes than in using eggs, butter, flour, salt or pepper.

It sounds rather absurd to say so but, in a great many recipes, it is important that the wine should not taste. Why the extravagance of putting it in? the reader might ask. My answer would be that, if a dish tastes of salt, of pepper, of sugar, of cloves, of garlic, of onion, it means that you have put in too much. Obviously, a curry must taste of curry, but if tamarind predominates it is a bad curry. A chocolate *soufflé* must taste of chocolate, but the vanilla in the sugar is a supplementary taste, not the predominant one. In most dishes in which wine is an ingredient, the predominant taste should be that of the fish, bird, meat or fruit on which the dish is based. Only in something such as a *coq au vin* should the wine be as prominent as the chicken. Even then, it should, in my view, be the secondary taste, not the predominant one.

For this reason it is important for the cook to restrain him or herself in the use of wine. If the recipe calls for a glass, no good is done by using a bottle. And, when cooking with wine, it is important with most dishes to cook them for some time so that the wine is embodied into the other ingredients and does not taste like an extravagant afterthought.

This is even more true with spirits, and, except with something like *ananas au Kirsch*, where the liqueur is not cooked at all, any fieriness should be avoided. For this reason, where I use spirits in any recipe, I nearly always set fire to them before adding them to the dish and then cook the dish for a few minutes longer so that the spirit is absorbed.

As for the wine available for cooking: everything depends on your drinking habits. If you habitually drink wine – red or white – there is usually some left over which can be kept for cooking. Some cookery writers advocate pouring the remains of a bottle into a small bottle, corking it up and keeping it in a kitchen cupboard. As I tend to drink wine between meals as well as at them, I should find, if I went in for this practice, that the cupboard was usually bare. For me, if there is not a bottle open, it does no harm to open one: what I do not use for cooking can be very happily drunk before, during or after the meal.

From this it may be deduced that I am not in the habit of cooking with Château Laffite, Château d'Yquem or Krug. If you use wine in large quantities in a dish – which, as I have said, I am against – it may be obvious if you are using the less attractive products of Australia, Cyprus or Algeria. But if you use wine modestly, I defy any of the greatest experts to tell whether you have used a ten-and-sixpenny Mâcon or a £5 Romanée-Conti. If a dish calls for a glass of Champagne and you do not happen to have any on tap, buy a quarter-bottle.

Wines, when opened, will keep for several days – as far as cooking is concerned. If you are lucky enough to have a bottle of first-growth claret, don't be so foolish as to ask it to keep: drink it up. But, if you have half a bottle of swigging wine left over from a meal, cork it up, if it be white put it in the refrigerator, and it is quite good enough for cooking purposes for the next week.

Fortified wines present no problem. Sherry remains perfectly good for weeks. Vintage port loses some of its *bouquet* after a day or two, but a tawny port, which I should use for cooking, keeps perfectly well in the kitchen cupboard. Madeira keeps more or less for ever. Marsala or muscatel are only fit, in my view, for the kitchen cupboard. Brandy, whisky, gin and liqueurs get no better, no worse, with keeping. If you need some exotic liqueur for a dish and are unlikely to get through a bottle in two years, I should buy a miniature or a large measure from the 'local'.

I must not give the impression that any old wine will do. When I say red, I mean claret or Burgundy – at a pinch, Rhône, Spanish or Portuguese. When I say claret, I mean claret; when Burgundy, Burgundy. When I say 'dry white' I mean a dry white; when I say Sauterne, I mean a sweet white.

Apart from straight cooking with wines, there are two very important processes in which wine is involved: marinating and poaching. Wine in a marinade softens the meat and, like the herbs that usually accompany it, gives it a flavour. (The somewhat similar operation of macerating fruit gives the fruit the flavour of the wine and brings out the fruit's juices but is not designed to soften it.) Poaching in a *court-bouillon* made with wine adds enormously to a fish's flavour: try poaching in plain water and then in a *court-bouillon* to see the difference.

As for *flambé*-ing, it is not a process I am very keen on. There are some dishes, such as *figues flambées*, where the cooking process is done by the burning spirit. I am against the restaurant habit of *flambage* for *flambage*'s sake: all it produces is unnecessary heat, a smell of methylated spirits and, if the waiter isn't careful, singed eyebrows all round. Cooking, in my opinion, should be done in a kitchen.

NOTE Measurements in the recipes have been given in both English and American systems (hence **E** and **A**). Unless specified otherwise, the recipes are designed to feed four people.

Terrine de Saumon

1 lb. salmon	milk
salt and pepper	**E** ¼ lb., **A** ½ cup butter
1 shallot	2 egg-yolks
1 bayleaf	1 pinch mace
2 glasses sherry	flour and water
E 1 cup, **A** 1¼ cups breadcrumbs	

Cut two thirds of the salmon into pieces and marinate them with the shallot, chopped, and the bayleaf in the sherry in a cool place overnight (covered). Soak the breadcrumbs in milk, soften the butter and mash up the rest of the salmon with them, adding the egg-yolks, mace and seasoning to make a forcemeat. Butter a *terrine* and put in a layer of the forcemeat, on that put some pieces of salmon and continue, ending with a layer of forcemeat on top. Strain on the sherry. Put the lid on the *terrine*. Seal it with a paste of flour and water. Cook for 2 hrs in a *bain-marie* in a slow oven (300–325° F., Reg. 1–2). Let it get cold. Serve as a first course without any accompanying sauce.

Terrine de Faisan

1 pheasant	2 cloves garlic
½ glass brandy	salt and pepper
½ glass Madeira	1 lb. pork (fat and lean)
1 glass white wine	1 small tin *foie gras*
parsley, tarragon, chives,	1 truffle
chervil, as available	bacon

Cut the meat off the breast and the thighs of the pheasant and marinate the pieces for 24 hrs in the brandy, Madeira and white wine with the herbs and the garlic chopped up. Grind up the pork and any pieces of meat remaining on the pheasant, together with its liver, so as to make a forcemeat. Season. Line the *terrine* with rashers of bacon. Put in a layer of the forcemeat, on that some pieces of the marinated pheasant, a thin layer of *foie gras*, some slivers of truffle. Continue the layers, finishing with a layer of forcemeat. Strain on the marinade. Cover with more rashers. Put on the lid of the *terrine*. Cook in a *bain-marie* in a slow oven (300–325° F., Reg. 1–2) for 1½ hrs. Let it get cold. Serve in the *terrine*.

Chicken Liver Pâté

1 lb. chicken livers	1 clove garlic
E 2 oz., **A** 4 tablespoons butter	1 glass brandy
¼ onion	

Chop the onion and garlic and *sautez* them in butter till they are soft – they should not colour. Wash, clean and dry the chicken livers. Add them to the onion and stir them about to cook all round. When they get soft, mash them with a fork. Heat the brandy in a spoon, set fire to it and stir it in. Put the chicken livers through a fine mill into a *terrine*. Cover and cook in a *bain-marie* in a slow oven (300–325° F., Reg. 1–2) for ½ hr. Cool with a weight on top. If you like, you can pour clarified butter on top. Serve in the *terrine*.

Marinated Herring

6 herrings	1 onion
E 1 pt, **A** 2½ cups water	a *bouquet garni*
E ½ pt, **A** 1¼ cups white wine	3 bayleaves
E ¼ pt, **A** ½ cup white wine vinegar	12 peppercorns
1 carrot	salt

Make a *court-bouillon* (p. 27) with the water, wine, vinegar, herbs, the carrot cut in slices and the onion cut in thick rings, the peppercorns and a little salt. Bring it to the boil, let it simmer for ½ hr and then get cold. Scale, clean and bone the herrings. If the fillets are very large, cut them in half. Put the herrings in the *court-bouillon* and bring them slowly to the boil. Let them simmer until the herrings get soft – about ¼ hr. Let them get cool in the liquor. Remove the herrings to a glass dish and strain some of the cooking-liquor over them. Garnish with some of the onion rings and a few thin half-slices of lemon.

Marinated Mackerel

The above recipe may very well be applied to mackerel. It is perhaps better to use all wine and no wine vinegar, which is inclined to drown the subtler taste of mackerel.

Truites Marinées

Make a *court-bouillon* (p. 27) with white wine and water with some slices of onion, salt and peppercorns. Let it cool. Put some trout in the *court-bouillon* and bring it slowly to the boil. Simmer. It will take only a few minutes for the trout to be cooked. Let them cool in the liquor. Take them out and put them on a shallow earthenware dish. Strain over some of the cooking-liquor. Decorate with thin half-slices of lemon.

Cocktail Sauce

1 measure Heinz tomato ketchup
¼ measure dry sherry

½ measure Lee & Perrins'
    Worcestershire sauce

Mix the three ingredients in a glass and serve in the middle of a plate surrounded by oysters or clams.

Lobster Cocktail

1 lobster of about 1½ lb.
E ¼ pt double cream, **A** a good
    ½ cup heavy cream
half as much Heinz tomato
    ketchup

a liberal dash of Lee & Perrins'
    Worcestershire sauce
a liberal dash of dry sherry
some fresh grapefruit- or
    lemon-juice
paprika

Cook the lobster. Let it get cold and cut it into small pieces. Mix the claw meat, the tail meat and the coral so that everyone gets his fair share. Make the cocktail sauce with the other ingredients and stir it into the lobster. Put some shredded lettuce in glasses, spoon on some of the lobster mixture. Decorate with paprika,

Note: the sauce and the lobster should be mixed just before serving; otherwise the sauce sinks to the bottom of the glass. They can be prepared in advance and kept separately in a cold place.

I have had the sauce made with brandy and even with whisky, but I still prefer sherry.

Mussels in Wine Vinaigrette*

Cook some mussels as if for *moules marinière* (p. 51). Keep the liquor for a fish soup. Take the mussels out of their shells when they get cool. Make a *vinaigrette* with one part of a dry white wine to three of olive oil, with salt, pepper and chopped herbs – garlic, parsley, tarragon and chives. Cover the mussels with this dressing and serve as part of a mixed *hors d'œuvre*.

Beetroot in Wine Vinaigrette*

Cook tiny beetroots very gently either in water on a low flame or in the oven. When they are done, remove their skins and let them get cold. Make a dressing with one part of dry white wine to three of olive oil, with salt and pepper, and pour it over the beetroots. Sprinkle on a lot of coarsely chopped fresh parsley.

* I suppose it is rather dotty to say 'wine vinaigrette' but I dislike the expression 'French dressing'.

Mushrooms in Wine Vinaigrette*

Wash and dry some fresh, uncooked button mushrooms, cut off the stalks (keeping them for a stew), and slice them very finely vertically. Chop some garlic finely and some parsley. Mix in with the mushrooms. Season with salt and freshly ground pepper. Pour over them a dressing made of one part of white wine to three of olive oil. Serve as part of a mixed *hors d'œuvre*.

Fondue

1 clove garlic	**E** 3 oz., **A** 6 tablespoons butter
¼ bottle dry white wine	4 eggs
½ lb. Gruyère	1 glass Kirsch

Chop the garlic finely and cook it in the wine till the wine is reduced by half. Melt the cheese (it should be real Gruyère, not Emmenthal) in some of the butter over a low flame. Beat the eggs (not whip – just beat to mix) and pour them over the cheese. Add the rest of the butter and continue to stir, keeping the flame low. Strain in the wine gradually. When all the ingredients are amalgamated, stir in the Kirsch. Cook for a little longer. Serve with bits of hot toast which you dip in the pot on the end of a fork. (Not very hygienic.)

Fonds d'Artichauts à la Grecque

Cook some globe artichokes in water for about 10 mins. Remove the leaves and the choke and trim the bottoms. Put them

* See footnote on page 15.

in a large flat fireproof dish and cover them with a mixture of equal parts of white wine, water and oil, with salt, lemon-juice, coriander seeds, peppercorns, thyme and a bayleaf. Let them cook in a slow oven (300–325° F., Reg. 1–2) for ½ hr and then cool in the cooking liquor. Serve very cold in the same dish, first pouring off some of the cooking liquor.

Poireaux à la Grecque

Trim some leeks and poach them in salted water for about 15 mins. Cut them in 2-in. pieces and cook them as in the preceding recipe for *fonds d'artichauts à la grecque*.

Melon au Porto

I give a recipe for melon with port in the pudding chapter because I like it at the end of a meal. But many people like to begin with melon. Let those who do, see p. 128.

Œufs Pochés Bourguignonne

2 glasses Burgundy
2 glasses water
1 small onion
1 clove garlic
bouquet garni
salt and pepper
nutmeg

eggs
E 1 dessertspoon, **A** 1 tablespoon butter
E 1 dessertspoon, **A** 1 tablespoon flour
bread

Slice the onion coarsely, divide the garlic in two and boil them in the Burgundy and water with the *bouquet* and seasoning for 10 mins. Take out the onion, etc., with a perforated spoon, and in the liquid poach as many eggs as you want. Take them out and keep them hot. Reduce the liquor, strain and, if you have more than you need, pour the surplus away. Thicken the remainder with some *beurre manié* made with the butter and flour. Fry some pieces of bread in butter. Put the eggs on the bread and pour over the sauce.

Jambon Persillé

1 lb. **E** gammon, **A** ham	1 bottle white Burgundy
1 knuckle of veal	1 teaspoon wine vinegar
2 calves' feet	salt and pepper
thyme, bay, tarragon, parsley, chervil	2 bunches parsley

Soak the gammon overnight. Cook it in boiling water for an hour. Put it under a running cold tap. Then put it in a large pot with the veal knuckle, the calves' feet, the herbs (chopped), salt and pepper and most of the wine, and cook till the gammon is quite soft and can be mashed with a fork. Mix lean and fat together and press down into a bowl or pudding-basin. Clarify the cooking liquor to make a clear jelly. Strain. Add the parsley, chopped, the vinegar and the rest of the wine. Pour it on to the gammon and let it get cold. Serve it in the bowl or turn it out, as you wish. If you serve it in the bowl, it should be a better looking one than an ordinary pudding-basin : a glass dish looks best.

Soups

Consommé au Madère

E 2 qts, A 5 pts water
E 1½ lb. shin of beef,
 A 1½ lb. stew meat
a chicken carcase
2 large carrots
1 turnip
2 leeks

1 onion
cloves
2 egg-whites and shells
salt
Madeira
lemon
cheese straws

Boil 1 lb. beef and three quarters of the chicken carcase in the water, salted, and skim frequently. Add the carrots, turnip and leeks and the onion, whole, with two or three cloves in it. Simmer, skimming frequently, for 4–5 hrs. Let it get nearly cold, skim, strain.

Take as much of the liquid as you need for your *consommé* and put it in a saucepan. Pound the rest of the beef and the chicken carcase, stir in the egg-whites and a little stock. Add this and the egg-shells to the saucepan and bring to the boil. Simmer for an hour, skimming the grease from the top. Strain into a tureen. Correct the seasoning. Add a glass of Madeira. Serve with a piece of lemon and some cheese straws.

Some like a few drops of chili sherry.

Chili Sherry

Half fill a large, wide-necked jar with hot chillies. Fill up with dry sherry – South African Mymering does well. Screw on the top. Keep for 3 to 6 months before using, shaking when you can remember. When ready, transfer a few chillies to a bitters bottle and fill up with sherry. Considered by some an insult to a well-made soup, but not by me.

Turtle Soup

Escoffier says: 'take a turtle weighing from 120 to 180 lb., and let it be very fleshy and full of life'. I say, buy as many tins of Lusty's turtle soup as you need. If you find it more concentrated than you like, thin it down with a little *consommé*. Bring it nearly to the boil. Add some sherry or Madeira. Taste at this stage to see if you have added enough: it is a mistake to add more cold sherry or Madeira at the table.

Hare Soup

hare carcase	**E** 2½ pts, **A** 6 cups water
flour	**E** 1 dessertspoon, **A** 1 table-
2 onions	spoon redcurrant jelly

1 carrot	1 teaspoon sugar
bouquet garni	1 glass port
E 1 dessertspoon, **A** 1 tablespoon butter	salt and pepper

Chop the onions and slice the carrot and cook them in butter. Cut up the hare carcase (which should include the legs), flour the pieces and brown them with the vegetables. Add the water and the *bouquet* and cook gently until the hare meat falls away from the bones. Remove the bones and the *bouquet*. Put the hare and vegetables through a fine mill. Strain on the cooking liquor. Add the jelly, sugar, port and salt and pepper. Cook for another 5 or 10 mins. Taste and add more port, salt or pepper, if required. Serve with *croûtons*.

Pheasant Soup

E 1 dessertspoon, **A** 1 tablespoon butter	1 pheasant carcase
E 2½ pts, **A** 6 cups water	2 onions
salt and pepper	sherry

The pheasant carcase must have a reasonable amount of meat still on it – the bones alone will not make a very good soup, though they will make adequate stock.

Chop the onions and cook them in butter. Break up the pheasant and add the pieces to the onion. Cover with water. Season. Simmer for several hours, skimming off the fat. Remove the bones. Put the pheasant meat and onion through a mill, strain on the cooking liquor, bring to the boil and skim. Add as much sherry, salt and pepper as you need. If you have a little of the breast of pheasant left over, chop it up and stir it into the soup as a garnish.

Chicken Soup

the carcase of a roast chicken with a good deal of meat still on it
1 onion
E 1 dessertspoon, **A** 1 tablespoon butter

E 2½ pts, **A** 6 cups water
salt and pepper
sherry
about ½ cup cream

Chop the onion and cook it in butter. Break up the carcase and add it. Toss the pieces with the onion, then add the water. Season. Simmer a couple of hours till the flesh comes quite easily from the bones. Remove the bones and put the flesh through a mill. Strain on the cooking-liquor. Bring to the boil and skim. Correct the seasoning and add some sherry, tasting so as not to overdo it – chicken, not sherry, must predominate. Add some cream and do not let the soup boil again.

Wild Duck Soup

1 small wild duck (e.g. widgeon)
flour
1 onion
E 1 dessertspoon, **A** 1 tablespoon butter

a *bouquet garni*
2 glasses port
E 2½ pts, **A** 6 cups water

Cut the duck into pieces and flour them. Include the liver. Chop the onion and cook it in butter. Add the duck and brown it. Add 1 glass port. Add about half the water, bring to the boil and simmer gently for at least two hours. Pick the flesh off the bones and put it through a mill. Strain on the cooking-liquor. Add the rest of the water. Season. Bring to the boil. Simmer and skim. Add the other glass of port and bring nearly to the boil. Serve with thin slices of French bread baked hard in the oven.

(If you like a thicker soup, make a *roux* with butter and flour, mix in some of the soup gradually and stir into the rest of the soup. The flour must be well and slowly cooked to avoid the taste of raw flour, and the soup must be stirred in very gradually to avoid making lumps.)

Bisque de Homard

E 1½ pts, **A** 4 cups fish-stock	1 tablespoon brandy
1 small lobster	1 glass white wine
1 onion	salt and pepper
parsley, thyme, bayleaf	½ cup boiled rice
about 2 tablespoons butter	2–3 tablespoons cream

Cut up the lobster – cutting off its head with a chopper or driving a pick into its head kills it instantaneously, and the former method is the easier. The tail should be cut across in pieces about an inch thick. Chop the carrot, onion and parsley and *sautez* them in a good half of the butter with the thyme and bayleaf. Add the pieces of lobster. Shake to cook them all round. Heat the brandy in a spoon, set fire to it and pour it over the lobster. Add the white wine, salt and pepper and cook to reduce the liquid. Add **E** ½ pt/**A** 1 cup fish-stock and cook with the lid on for 10–15 mins. Take out the pieces of lobster, remove the meat, dice and keep warm. Strain off the cooking-liquor and keep. Remove the thyme and bayleaf and pound the rest, shells included, in a mortar. Rub through a sieve. Put the rice – which should be somewhat overcooked and not too dry – through the sieve. Add the cooking liquor and the rest of the fish-stock. Bring to the boil. Simmer. Strain. Add the diced pieces of lobster, and stir in the rest of the butter, cut in small pieces, and the cream.

Cherry Soup

1 lb. red cherries	**E** 3 tablespoons, **A** 4½ table-
3 cloves	spoons granulated sugar
small piece cinnamon	**E** 2 pts, **A** 5 cups water
lemon-juice	1–1½ tablespoons **E** cornflour,
zest of lemon	**A** corn starch
	2 glasses claret

Cook the cherries with the cloves, cinnamon, sugar, lemon and water. When they are done, remove the stones. Take out the spices. Put half the cherries through a fine sieve and return to the cooking liquor. Dissolve the **E** cornflour/**A** corn starch in the wine and add to the cherry liquor. Cook for 15 mins., adding more sugar if necessary (the quantity depends, of course, on the sweetness of the cherries). Add the whole cherries and serve hot. You can have a sauceboat of sour cream served separately. The soup can also be served cold.

A refinement is to break the cherry stones, take out the kernels and let them infuse in the wine. The wine is then strained off and the kernels discarded.

Beer Soup

E 2 tablespoons, **A** 3 tablespoons flour	**E** ¼ pt double cream, **A** ½ cup heavy cream
E 2 tablespoons, **A** 3 tablespoons butter	salt and pepper
E 2 pts, **A** 5 cups lager (draught, if available)	a pinch of powdered cinnamon
E 1 dessertspoon, **A** 1 tablespoon sugar	Melba toast

Make a light *roux* with the butter and flour, cooking it slowly and mixing it well. Gradually work in the beer. Add the salt and pepper, the sugar and cinnamon, bring to the boil and simmer. Add the cream, bring back to the boil and pour at once on to a piece of hot Melba toast in each soup plate.

Kidney Soup

E 1 oz., **A** 2 tablespoons butter   1 veal kidney
E 1 oz., **A** 4 tablespoons flour   1 glass Madeira
E 2 pts, **A** 5 cups beef-stock or *consommé*

Make a *roux* with the butter and flour. Work in gradually some heated stock. Add the rest of the stock and bring to the boil. Blanch and skin the kidney and put it through a sieve or a very fine mill. Add to the soup and cook for 15 mins. Strain, season, reheat and add the Madeira. Cook for a few more minutes so that the taste of the Madeira is incorporated with that of the soup.

Chicken-Liver Soup

E 1 oz., **A** 2 tablespoons butter   ½ lb. chicken livers
E 1 oz., **A** 4 tablespoons flour   1 glass Madeira
E 2 pts, **A** 5 cups chicken or veal stock

Make a *roux* with the butter and flour. Gradually add the stock and bring to the boil. Rub the chicken livers through a sieve and add to the stock. Bring to the boil and simmer for 15 mins.

Strain. Correct the seasoning. Add the Madeira. Bring to the boil. Serve very hot.

Some add as a garnish a few small pieces of chicken liver which have been tossed very quickly in butter and the butter drained off, but if they are hard on the outside the soup is better without them.

Peanut Soup

½ lb. shelled peanuts
½ large onion
E 1 tablespoon, **A** 1½ tablespoons butter
E ¾ pt, **A** 2 cups chicken stock

E ¾ pt, **A** 2 cups milk
pepper
1 tablespoon cream
1 glass sherry

Skin the nuts and pulverize them. (I do it in a Moulinex.) Chop the onion and cook it in the butter till it is soft but not coloured. Stir in the nuts and cook for a minute, stirring with a wooden spoon. Add the chicken stock. Bring to the boil and simmer for ¾ hr. Put through a mill – it may need a medium one, then a fine one. Add the pepper (probably no salt). Add the milk and bring to the boil. Add the cream and sherry. Stir to mix them in but do not boil again.

Fish

Court-Bouillon

Before giving a chapter of recipes for cooking fish, it might be as well to say what is meant by *court-bouillon* which will be mentioned in many of the recipes. Fish poached or boiled in plain water may taste all right but it will taste only of itself. The object of making a *court-bouillon* is to impart some flavour to the water which, in turn, will impart its flavour to the fish. The usual ingredients of a *court-bouillon* are onions, carrots, herbs, salt and pepper, and wine or vinegar, sometimes both.

The quantity to be made depends on the size of the fish and on the size of the cooking utensil (a fish-kettle is best for cooking on top of the stove). The pot should be only a little larger than the fish, and the liquid in the pot should just cover the fish. A fish-kettle should have a perforated rack with handles so that the fish, when cooked, can be lifted out whole, avoiding the risk of breaking it up by trying to get it out with a couple of forks or even fish slices.

To **E** a quart/**A** 5 cups of water allow **E** ½ pt/**A** 1¼ cups white wine or **E** ¼ pt/**A** ½ cup white wine with a tablespoonful of wine vinegar. With this quantity use a medium-sized onion, cut in rings, two carrots, cut in slices, a *bouquet garni* (including a bayleaf), some salt and 12 peppercorns. Bring the *court-bouillon* gently to the boil and let it simmer for 30–40 mins. Let it get cold. When ready to cook the fish, put it into the cold *court-bouillon* and bring it gently to the boil. Simmer till the fish is cooked. If it is to be eaten cold, let it cool in the *court-bouillon*.

Some cooks use half water, half wine, but I think that extravagant. Beware of putting in too much vinegar: the fish should not taste of vinegar.

For cooking turbot, Escoffier advocates using **E** ½ pt/**A** 1¼ cups milk to **E** a quart/**A** 5 cups of water, no vegetables or herbs but just a slice of lemon – plus salt and pepper, of course.

There are occasions, as will be seen, when red wine is used instead of white: omit the vinegar.

Filets de Sole au Vin Blanc

8 fillets of sole
¼ bottle white wine
salt and pepper

E 1 tablespoon, **A** 1½ tablespoons butter

E 1 dessertspoon, **A** 1 tablespoon flour

Butter a fireproof dish and lay in the fillets. Season, cover with wine. Cook in a moderate oven (350° F., Reg. 4) with a piece of greaseproof paper on top for about 20–30 mins. Take the fillets out and keep them warm. Reduce the cooking-liquor in a saucepan. Correct the seasoning. Add, a small piece at a time, some *beurre manié* – the flour worked into half the butter – to thicken the sauce. Add the rest of the butter in small pieces. Pour this sauce over the fillets and put the dish under a grill for a minute.

The variations on this recipe depend on the wines you have available. It can be done with a somewhat characterless cheap white wine, in which case the fish is the thing. But the character of the wine does come through very clearly in the finished product, and if one had the remains of a bottle of Château d'Yquem to spare one would get a very superior dish to one made of white Rioja. Something like a Muscadet is perhaps a happy compromise. With an Yquem or any other less grand sweet wine a few skinned, depipped grapes make an elegant garnish.

Note: I give this recipe and the ones which follow for fillets of sole, as I think they are much more manageable in a private house than whole soles; but the recipes do also, of course, apply to whole soles.

Sole au Vermouth

Follow the recipe for *sole au vin blanc*, but, instead of using white wine, use a dry vermouth.

Some prefer to use a mixture of vermouth and fish-stock.

Fillets of Sole in Cyder

Same as *sole au vin blanc* but using cyder – not the fizzy kind – instead of white wine. As with the vermouth recipe above, you can use half fish-stock, half cyder. I favour some chopped shallots in the earthenware dish, the sauce strained and reduced and thickened with *beurre manié*.

Sole Amiral

Filets de sole au vin blanc garnished with button onions and button mushrooms, cooked in butter and drained, with the sauce poured over all the ingredients.

Sole Argenteuil

Sole au vin blanc garnished with asparagus tips.

Fillets de Sole Bénédictine

Fillets of sole *au vin blanc* arranged round a mound of *brandade de morue* (salt cod, garlic, olive oil, cream).

Sole Claremont

Prepare *filets de sole au vin blanc* (p. 28) in the usual way. While they are cooking, skin two tomatoes, squeeze out the juice and chop the flesh. Chop some parsley finely. When you have finished the sauce, stir in the tomato and parsley and cook them for a few minutes in the sauce. Pour over the fillets (unstrained). Serve with diamond-shaped *croûtons*.

Sole Czarine

Sole au vin blanc (p. 28) with some grated horseradish and some cream mixed into the sauce. Should be served with rounds of toast spread with caviar.

Sole Fines Herbes

Sole au vin blanc (p. 28) with chopped parsley, tarragon and chives sprinkled on top.

Sole Lydia

Sole au vin blanc (p. 28) garnished with shrimps and asparagus tips heated in the sauce. Glaze under a grill.

Sole Marseillaise

Sole au vin blanc (p. 28) with a pinch of saffron added while the sauce is reducing.

Sole au Vin Rouge

The procedure for making *filets de sole au vin rouge* is exactly the same as in the recipe for *sole au vin blanc* (p. 28) but using red wine instead of white. A fairly light wine is preferable to a heavy, coarse one. With some wines the sauce is improved at the reduction stage by a squeeze of lemon juice.

Garnish the dish with *croûtons* fried in butter – diamond-shaped look best.

Sole Bordelaise

Butter a fireproof dish and sprinkle in a thin bed of chopped shallots. On this lay the fillets of sole. Proceed as in the previous recipe, using a claret. Strain the reduced sauce over the fillets and sprinkle on some chopped parsley.

Sole Bourguignonne

Make a dish of *filets de sole au vin rouge*, using a Burgundy. While they are cooking, cook some button mushrooms and button onions in butter. Arrange them on the dish with the fillets and pour over the sauce.

Sole au Chambertin

As for *sole au vin rouge*, using, properly, Chambertin, though most cooks cheat and use whatever Burgundy is available. While the fillets are cooking in the oven, cut another sole into *goujons*: that is to say, skin and fillet it and, with a pair of scissors, cut it into pieces the size of large whitebait. Dip them in milk, roll them in flour and fry them in deep fat. When the poached sole are cooked, strain the sauce over them and garnish with the *goujons*. The contrast between the crisp bits of sole and the fillets in the rich red wine sauce is very pleasant and rather more exciting than *croûtons*.

Sole au Champagne

8 fillets of sole	butter
4 mushrooms	2 egg-yolks
1 onion	cream
salt and pepper	truffle
½ bottle Champagne	pastry crescents

Take the skin, bones and head of the sole, the mushrooms and onion, chopped, the salt and pepper and the Champagne and cook them together for ½ hr. Strain and reduce. Cook the fillets in butter (about 10 mins. slow cooking) and take them out with a perforated fish slice (to drain off the butter). Keep them warm on a serving-dish. Thicken the sauce with the egg-yolks and a little butter. Add a little cream. Pour this sauce over the fillets. Decorate with a thin slice of truffle on each fillet and some little puff-pastry crescents.

Sole Archiduc

Cook fillets of sole in some fish-stock to which you have added equal but small quantities of whisky, port and Madeira. Take out the fillets when cooked and keep them hot. Reduce the stock. Strain. Thicken with *beurre manié* and cream. Pour this sauce over the fillets and decorate each with a thin slice of truffle. You should garnish the dish with alternate little mounds of *macédoine de légumes* and crescents of puff pastry.

Sole Bercy

Butter a fireproof dish. Cover the bottom with a thin layer of chopped shallots and chopped parsley. Lay fillets of sole on this mixture. Cover with a mixture of white wine and fish-stock. Season. Cover with greaseproof paper. Cook in a moderate oven (350° F., Reg. 4) for about ½ hr. Take out the fillets and keep them warm. Reduce the cooking-liquor in a saucepan. Strain. Thicken the sauce with *beurre manié*, pour it over the fillets and put the dish under a grill for a minute.

Sole Bonne Femme

8 fillets of sole	salt and pepper
8 shallots	1 glass white wine
16 mushrooms	½ cup fish-stock
parsley	½ cup fish *velouté*

Fish *velouté*: make a *roux* with butter and flour. Add a little fish-stock, whisking so that it is not lumpy. Keep it hot in a *bain-marie* till needed.

Butter a fireproof dish. Chop the shallots, parsley and half the mushrooms and spread them over the bottom of the dish. Put the fillets on this bed. Cover with white wine and fish-stock, season and cook in a moderate oven (350° F., Reg. 4) for about ½ hr. Cook the remaining mushrooms in butter. Keep the fillets warm while you reduce the cooking-liquor. Add it to the fish *velouté*, whisking well. Put a mushroom on each fillet and strain over the sauce. Glaze under the grill.

Sole Dieppoise

8 fillets of sole
E ½ pt, A 1¼ cups cooked shrimps
12 mussels
E ¼ pt, A a good ½ cup white wine
E ¼ pt, A a good ½ cup fish-stock
E ¼ lb., A ½ cup butter
12 mushrooms
beurre manié

Butter a fireproof dish and put in the fillets. Open the mussels (as in *moules marinière* on p. 51). Add to the fillets their liquid, the white wine and enough fish-stock just to cover them. Cook in a moderate oven (350° F., Reg. 4) for about ½ hr.

Sautez the mushrooms in butter, add the shrimps and mussels to heat them. Drain and keep them warm.

When the fillets are cooked, strain the cooking-liquor into a saucepan and reduce it. Thicken with a little *beurre manié*. Put the mushrooms, shrimps and mussels on to the sole and pour over the sauce. Glaze under a grill.

Sole Dugléré (hot)

8 fillets of sole	¼ bottle white wine
4 tomatoes	½ cup fish *velouté* (p. 35)
1 large onion	butter
parsley	lemon-juice
salt and pepper	

Skin the tomatoes and chop them coarsely. Chop the onion and parsley finely. Put them in a buttered fireproof dish and on them lay the fillets. Season. Add the white wine. Cook in a moderate oven (350° F., Reg. 4) for 20–30 mins. Take the fillets out and keep them warm. Reduce the cooking-liquor and thicken it with the fish *velouté*. Add a little butter and a few drops of lemon-juice. Pour the sauce over the sole without straining it.

Sole Dugléré (cold)

Cook the fillets with the tomato, onion, parsley and white wine, as in the preceding recipe. Take out the fillets and let them get cold. Reduce, without straining, the cooking-liquor. Do not add fish *velouté* or butter, though you can add the lemon-juice. Let the (unstrained) sauce also get cold. When cold, stir in some thick mayonnaise and spread the resulting sauce over the fillets. Serve very cold.

Sole François Ier

Poach fillets of sole in white wine on a bed of chopped onion, tomato, mushrooms and parsley. Reduce the cooking-liquor and pour it, unstrained, over the fillets.

Sole Palace

8 fillets of sole	1 liqueur glass brandy
6 shallots	¼ bottle white wine
a bunch of tarragon	2 tomatoes
salt and pepper	8 mushrooms

Butter a fireproof dish and in it make a bed of chopped shallots and tarragon. On this lay the fillets. Season. Add the brandy and enough wine to cover the fillets. Cook in a moderate oven (350° F., Reg. 4), covered, for 20–30 mins. Reduce the sauce. Peel and slice the tomatoes. *Sautez* the mushrooms in butter and drain them. Decorate the fillets with the slices of tomato and the mushrooms. Pour on the sauce and glaze under a grill.

Sole sur Plat

Poach fillets of sole in white wine and fish-stock with a few chopped shallots. Reduce the sauce, thicken with butter and pour it back on to the fillets in the dish. Glaze.

Sole au Foie Gras

per person
1 sole (skinned but not
    filleted)
1 glass Champagne
salt and pepper

1 slice *foie gras*
cream
sauce hollandaise

Poach the sole in a moderate oven (350° F., Reg. 4) in Champagne. When it is cooked – about ½ hr – take it out and, with a sharp knife, make a slit down the backbone. Slip in the knife sideways to loosen the top fillets. Cut out as much of the backbone as you can with a knife or scissors. Replace the backbone by some *foie gras*. Reduce the cooking liquor. Season and stir into it some cream and some *sauce hollandaise*. (This cannot be done at great heat.) Pour the sauce over the sole and glaze under a fierce grill.

This recipe comes from Monsieur Laporte of the Relais de Parme, Biarritz.

Sole Hongroise

8 fillets of sole
1 tablespoon chopped
    onion
butter
paprika
3–4 tablespoons white wine

fish-stock
2 tomatoes
salt and pepper
2–3 tablespoons
    cream
lemon-juice

Cook the onion in butter without letting it brown. Stir in some paprika. Add the wine and a little fish-stock. Peel the

tomatoes, squeeze out the juice and chop the flesh coarsely.
Add this to the other ingredients, season and cook for 8 mins.
Butter a fireproof dish and put the fillets in it. Cover them with
the onion and tomato mixture and, if necessary, add a little
more fish-stock. Poach in a moderate oven (350° F., Reg. 4),
covered, for about ½ hr. Pour off the cooking-liquor and reduce
it. Add some cream and lemon-juice and pour this sauce back
over the fillets.

Sole Newburg

Prepare a small lobster *à la Newburg*, as on p. 53. Cut the tail
into 16 pieces. Poach 8 fillets of sole in a mixture of white wine
and fish-stock. Cut the remains of the lobster meat into dice
and mix them into the Newburg sauce. Put two pieces of
lobster on to each fillet of sole and pour over the Newburg
sauce.

Sole Persane

Exactly as above but colour the sauce with a good deal of
paprika and mix in a small red pimento, cut in dice. Serve with
a pilaf rice into which you can, if you want a striking colour
contrast, mix some powdered saffron.

Sole Polignac

8 fillets of sole	**E** ¼ pt, **A** a good ½ cup white
3 mushrooms	wine
butter	**E** 2 tablespoons, **A** 3 table-
salt and pepper	spoons *fish velouté* (p. 35)
	1 truffle (optional)

Cook the mushrooms in very little butter. Pour the butter and the mushroom juice into a fireproof dish. Put in the fillets. Season. Add the white wine and poach, covered, in a slow oven (300–325° F., Reg. 1–2). Chop the mushrooms finely and cut the optional truffle very finely *julienne*. When the fillets are cooked, take them out and keep them warm. Reduce the cooking-liquor. Thicken with the fish *velouté* and a little butter. Add the mushrooms and truffles and pour this sauce over the fillets. Glaze under a grill.

Sole Délices de Luçat

8 fillets of sole	½ lb. tomatoes
butter	2 glasses of Pouilly Fuissé
salt and pepper	**E** ¼ pt double cream, **A** ½ cup
½ lb. mushrooms	heavy cream

Butter a fireproof dish and in it put the fillets, folded in half. Season. Chop the mushrooms and cover the fillets with them. Peel and *concassez* the tomatoes and spread them on the mushrooms. Add the wine. Cook in a hot oven (400° F., Reg. 6) for about 15 mins. Take out the fillets and keep them warm. Add the cream to the dish and let the sauce thicken. Replace the fillets in the dish and serve.

From the Château de Saran, Épernay.

Haddock Marcel

4 steaks of fresh haddock	6 mushrooms
E 2 oz., **A** 4 tablespoons butter	½ lemon
salt and pepper	2 glasses dry white wine
2 tomatoes	parsley and shallots

Put the haddock steaks in a buttered fireproof dish. Season. Cut up the butter into little pieces and put them on the fish. Pour in the wine. *Concassez* the tomatoes and add them, together with the mushrooms, sliced, and the lemon cut in slices. Cover with greaseproof paper and cook in a hot oven (400° F., Reg. 6) for 20–25 mins. Sprinkle with parsley and chopped shallots and serve in the dish in which it cooked.

Maquereau au Vin Rouge

E 1 dessertspoon, **A** 1 tablespoon butter	water
	sliced onion
E 1 dessertspoon, **A** 1 tablespoon flour	*bouquet garni*
	parsley
4 small mackerel	½ bottle red wine

Make a *court-bouillon* (p. 27), using equal quantities of red wine and water, and the onion and *bouquet garni*. Clean and wash the mackerel, cut them in half longitudinally and remove the back-bone. You are left with two fillets from each fish. Bring the *court-bouillon* to the boil – you need only enough to cover the fillets. Put the fillets in and let them simmer for 12–15 mins. Take them out and keep them hot in some of their cooking-liquor; strain and reduce the rest. Thicken the sauce with some *beurre manié* made from the butter and flour. Drain the fillets and put them on a serving-dish. Pour the sauce over them. Decorate with sprigs of crisply fried parsley.

Note: very thick fillets might take a little longer.

Rougets sur Plat

4 red mullet	¼ bottle white wine
olive oil	breadcrumbs
1 onion	lemon-juice
parsley	

Oil a fireproof dish. Sprinkle in some chopped onion and parsley. Put in the red mullet and add the white wine. Cook in a fairly hot oven (375° F., Reg. 5), basting well or turning the fish over at half-time – after about ¼ hr. While the fish are cooking, heat some breadcrumbs (bread dried in the oven and rolled out with a rolling-pin) in some olive oil. Dry them on blotting paper. Take the fish out of their dish, sprinkle on the breadcrumbs and squeeze on some lemon-juice.

Triglie alla Livornese

1 small red mullet per person	1 tomato
oil	1 tinned red pimento
1 small onion	2 capers
1 clove garlic	1 tablespoon dry white wine
salt and pepper	parsley
1 bayleaf	dash of brandy
4 small mushrooms (preserved in oil)	

Brown the onion in oil with the garlic, salt, pepper and bayleaf. Flour the red mullet and cook it slowly in oil, turning it over from time to time. Slice the mushrooms and cook them in a little oil with the pimento, chopped, the tomato, peeled and *concassée*, and the capers, chopped finely. Add the wine and reduce. Add a little chopped parsley and the dash of brandy. When the red mullet is cooked, take it out of the pan with as little of the oil as possible, put it on a plate and pour the sauce over it.

Rougets Nantaise

Cook some chopped shallots in a little white wine with some *demi-glace* to make a *sauce nantaise*. Grill as many red mullet as you need and serve with a garnish of slices of lemon and this sauce either in a sauceboat or poured over the mullet.

Turbot

I personally think turbot is such a good fish that it does not need anything very complicated done to it. I don't think you can beat turbot, cooked in a *court-bouillon* (p. 27) and served with a *sauce hollandaise* or with an old-fashioned egg sauce. You can cook a large piece or you can have it cut in steaks. The same applies to brill, halibut, fresh haddock and John Dory. But since this book is about cooking with wine, I had better say that most of the sole recipes can be applied to smallish steaks of white fish. However, *turbotin bonne femme* does not quite follow the recipe for *sole bonne femme* so I give that recipe, as well as one for *turbotin fermière* and one for a cold turbot.

Turbotin Bonne Femme

E 1 dessertspoon, **A** 1 tablespoon chopped shallots

E 3 oz., **A** 1 cup finely chopped mushrooms

E 3 tablespoons, **A** 4 tablespoons fish *velouté* (p. 35)

E 2 oz., **A** 4 tablespoons butter

a 2 to 3 lb. turbot

a pinch of chopped parsley

1 cup fish-stock

¼ bottle white wine

Cut the turbot down the back and loosen the fillets. Butter a fireproof dish and sprinkle in the shallots, parsley and mushrooms. Put in the turbot. Add the wine and the fish-stock. Cook in a slow oven (300–325° F., Reg. 1–2), basting frequently. When the turbot is cooked, take it out, skin it and keep it warm. In a saucepan, reduce the cooking-liquor by half, add the fish *velouté* and the butter gradually to thicken the sauce. Pour this sauce, unstrained, on to the fish and glaze under the grill.

Turbotin Fermière

4 turbot steaks	**E** $\frac{1}{2}$ oz., **A** 1 tablespoon butter, cut in pieces
2 shallots, finely chopped	
1 carrot, sliced	8 mushrooms, *sautés* in butter
$\frac{1}{2}$ onion, cut in rings	**E** 2 oz., **A** 4 tablespoons butter
parsley stalks, thyme, bayleaf	**E** 1 dessertspoon, **A** 1 table-
$\frac{1}{2}$ bottle white Burgundy	spoon flour

Butter an earthenware dish. Cover the bottom with the shallots, carrot, onion and herbs. Put in the turbot steaks. Add the wine. Put a little piece of butter on each steak. Poach in a gentle oven (330° F., Reg. 3), basting frequently. When the turbot is cooked – about $\frac{1}{2}$ hr – drain it and put it in a dish with the mushrooms round it. Strain and reduce the cooking-liquor by half. Thicken with *beurre manié* and the rest of the butter. Pour the sauce over the turbot and glaze under a grill. Some add cream to the sauce.

Turbotin au Champagne

1 small turbot	gelatine (optional)
salt and pepper	lettuce
½ bottle Champagne	hard-boiled eggs
court-bouillon (p. 27)	*mayonnaise* or *sauce verte*

Season the turbot and poach it in the oven in the Champagne with as much *court-bouillon* as you need nearly to cover it. (It is important not to have too big a cooking utensil so that there is not a surplus of liquid.) When it is cooked – about ½ hr – take it out, skin it and put it on a dish. Reduce the cooking-liquor. Strain it and clarify it and let it get cold. If it does not go to jelly, dissolve a little gelatine in hot water and add it – the less, the better. When the liquid does jellify, reheat it slightly so that it can be poured. Glaze the fish with the jelly and let it get cold. Garnish with hearts of lettuce and quarters of hard-boiled egg. Serve with a sauceboat of *mayonnaise* or *sauce verte*.

Saumon au Champagne

4 salmon steaks	**E** 1 dessertspoon, **A** 1 table-spoon flour
½ bottle Champagne	
a little *court-bouillon*, if necessary	**E** 1 dessertspoon, **A** 1 table-spoon butter
salt and pepper	
	parsley

Butter a fireproof dish. In it lay the salmon steaks. Season. Add the Champagne. If they are nearly covered add no *court-bouillon*, but add a little if they are not. Cover with buttered greaseproof paper and cook in a moderate oven (350° F., Reg. 4) till the steaks are done – about 20 mins. Take them out, drain them and keep them warm. Strain most of the cooking-liquor into a saucepan and cook fast to reduce. Mix the flour and butter together and add gradually to thicken the sauce. Pour the sauce over the fish – in the fireproof dish if it is a good-looking one. Decorate with sprigs of parsley, preferably crisply fried in butter.

The same dish can be made with a smallish whole sea-trout (*truite saumonée au Champagne*).

Salmon in White Wine

As in *Saumon au Champagne*, but using a dry white wine such as a Pouilly Fuissé or a Muscadet instead of Champagne.

Saumon Braisé Chambord

2 lb. salmon	**E** 2 oz., **A** 4 tablespoons butter
shallots, thyme, bayleaf,	**E** 1 oz., **A** 4 tablespoons flour
chopped mushrooms	*goujons* of sole ⎫
¾ bottle red wine	mushrooms ⎬ (Optional)
E ½ pt, **A** 1 cup fish-stock	truffle ⎭

Put the salmon in a fireproof dish on a bed of chopped mushrooms, herbs and shallots. Fill the dish two-thirds full with the wine and fish-stock, about two parts of wine to one of stock. Cook in a moderate oven (350° F., Reg. 4) for 20 to 30 mins. Make a *roux* with half the butter and the flour. Strain in the cooking-liquor and let it reduce. Thicken with the rest of the butter. Put the salmon (skinned) on a dish and pour some of the sauce over it. Serve the rest in a sauceboat.

A refinement is to decorate the fish with *goujons* of sole (sole cut across the fillet, little-finger size), egged and breadcrumbed and fried in oil, and with button mushrooms, tossed in butter, and slices of truffle, heated in red wine.

The same dish can be made with salmon steaks or with a small sea-trout (*truite saumonée*).

Saumon Dieppoise

4 salmon steaks
12 mussels
E ¼ pt, A ½ cup white wine
E ¼ pt, A ½ cup fish-stock
salt and pepper

12 mushrooms
E ½ pt, A 1¼ cups cooked shrimps
butter
flour

Butter a fireproof dish and put in the salmon steaks. Clean the mussels and open them as in *moules marinière* (p. 51). Add the mussel liquor, the wine and the fish-stock to the salmon. Season. Poach in a moderate oven (350° F., Reg. 4) for about 20 mins. *Sautez* the mushrooms in butter. When they are cooked, add the shrimps to heat through and the mussels (out of their shells) to reheat. When the salmon is cooked, remove the skin, strain off the cooking-liquor and reduce. Make a *roux* with butter and flour and whisk in the cooking-liquor to make a sauce. Put the mushrooms, shrimps and mussels on the salmon steaks and pour over the sauce. Glaze under a grill.

Truite Saumonée au Vin Blanc

1 sea-trout
salt and pepper
½ bottle dry white wine

butter
cucumber

Skin, clean and season the trout and put it in a buttered fireproof dish (preferably one which just fits it). Add the wine and cook in a slow oven (300–325° F., Reg. 1–2) for about ½ hr, basting frequently. Drain off the cooking-liquor and reduce it. Add some pieces of butter to thicken the sauce and pour it back over the fish. While the fish is cooking, cut a cucumber into lozenges or marbles and poach them in salted water. Drain them, toss them in butter and put them round the fish.

Matelote de Poisson

I cannot say I recommend a *matelote* and certainly would never buy fish for it. But if you own a river or lake which produces eel, carp, pike, tench, bream, perch, you may like to know how to make a *matelote*. You can use all, any, or a mixture of two or three.

Clean, scale, skin the fish, cut off the heads and cut them into pieces about 2 inches long. Put them in a saucepan with a large onion, chopped, 2 cloves garlic, 2 *bouquets garnis* (including bay-leaf), salt and peppercorns. Cover with ½ bottle coarse red wine and bring to the boil. Add **E** 2/**A** 3 tablespoonfuls brandy, heated and set alight. Simmer for about another 20 mins. Take out the pieces of fish and keep them warm. Strain and reduce the cooking-liquor. Thicken with *beurre manié* (blended butter and flour) and pour the sauce over the pieces of fish. Serve with *croûtons* of bread fried in butter or on thin slices of French bread made crisp in the oven.

Matelotes are sometimes made with white wine, the procedure being the same.

Waterzoi or Water Souchy

One never nowadays comes across a *waterzoi* or 'water souchy' in England. In the late eighteenth and early nineteenth centuries it was as famous at Greenwich as whitebait suppers. It is not unlike a *matelote*, being made of the same fish: eel, perch, pike, carp, tench – '*en somme*', as Montagné et Salles say, '*un genre de bouillabaisse de poissons d'eaux douces*'. I suppose it is Flemish in origin: André Simon calls it watersootje; Eliza Acton, water souchy (and I have found the verb 'to watersouch' in nineteenth-century memoirs); Escoffier has waterzoi.

Cut up the fish, whatever they may be – eel, pike, carp, etc. – in pieces as for a *matelote*. Take the heads and tails, carrots and onions, chopped, parsley roots, a *bouquet garni*, salt and peppercorns, put them in a saucepan and add two parts of water to one part of white wine. Bring to the boil and simmer for 45 mins. Strain this *court-bouillon* over the pieces of fish. Add **E** 1 oz./**A** 2 tablespoonfuls of butter for every pound of fish (when cut up). Cook very fast so that simultaneously the pieces of fish get cooked, the liquid reduces and the butter and *court-bouillon* combine (as in a *bouillabaisse*, but using butter instead of oil).

Traditionally served with slices of brown and white bread and butter.

Coquilles Saint-Jacques à la Crème

6 scallops	¼ cup **E** double/**A** heavy
olive oil	cream
flour	salt, pepper, cayenne
butter	6 button mushrooms

1 shallot, chopped	truffle (optional)
$\frac{1}{2}$ glass dry white wine	Parmesan cheese
lemon-juice	

Clean and cut up the scallops and marinate them for an hour in olive oil and lemon-juice. Take them out, flour them lightly and cook them in butter. Drain them. Put them back in four shells (you need six scallops for four people). Cook the shallot in butter, add the white wine and a few drops of lemon-juice. Reduce. Add the cream. Season. Slice the mushrooms and cook them in butter. Add them to the other pan and cook for a little. Add a little sliced truffle, if you are feeling extravagant. Pour over the scallops, grate on some Parmesan (not too much) and glaze under a fierce grill.

Coquilles Saint-Jacques au Vin Blanc

6 scallops	**E** 1 dessertspoon, **A** 1 table-
E $\frac{1}{2}$ pt, **A** $1\frac{1}{4}$ cups white wine	spoon flour
E $\frac{1}{2}$ pt, **A** $1\frac{1}{4}$ cups water	**E** 1 dessertspoon, **A** 1 table-
bouquet garni	spoon butter
salt and pepper	

Make a *court-bouillon* with the white wine, water, *bouquet*, salt and pepper. Simmer the scallops in it, the white parts first for 10 mins., then with the orange parts added for another 5 mins. Cut up the scallops and put them into four shells. Strain and reduce the cooking liquor – you may not need it all. Make a *roux* with the butter and flour. Whisk in some of the reduced cooking-liquor and pour the sauce over the scallops.

Moules Marinière

E 2 qts, **A** 5 pts mussels
2 shallots, finely chopped
1 tablespoon parsley, coarsely
  chopped
1 tablespoon celery leaves, coarsely
  chopped

1 teaspoon peppercorns
1 glass dry white wine
1 tablespoon butter
1 tablespoon parsley, finely
  chopped

Pick all the mussels over carefully and discard any doubtful-looking ones, for example with broken shells. Scrape them well and put them as you do so into a bucket under a cold tap. Change the water several times and, if you are energetic, give them a final scrub. Put them into a large shallow pan with the shallots, coarsely chopped parsley, celery leaves, the peppercorns, the white wine and half the butter. Cover. Cook over a brisk fire, shaking frequently. Remove the pan from the stove. Discard any mussels which have not opened. Put the good ones in a tureen to keep warm, after discarding the top shell. Strain the cooking-liquor into a saucepan and reduce, adding the rest of the butter. Stir in the finely chopped parsley and pour over the mussels.

Escoffier says of mussels: 'only used as a garnish'.

Moules Minute

E 2 qts, **A** 5 pts mussels
3 shallots
¼ heart of celery
3 teaspoons chopped parsley
pepper

1 glass Chablis
E 3 oz., **A** 6 tablespoons butter
1 tablespoon **E** double/**A**
  heavy cream

Clean the mussels well, discarding any doubtful ones. Put them in a pan with the shallots, celery and parsley, finely chopped, the pepper milled, the wine, butter and cream. Cook them over a high flame, shaking them, until they open. Remove the mussels, throw away the top shells and put the mussels in four soup plates to keep warm. Reduce the sauce and correct the seasoning and pour it over the mussels. Sprinkle with finely chopped parsley.

Each person needs a spoon, a fork and a finger-bowl.

Homard à l'Américaine

2 1–1½ lb. lobsters	1 clove garlic
1 tablespoon olive oil	1 glass white wine
1 tablespoon butter	½ cup fish-stock
1 tablespoon brandy	chopped parsley
2 tomatoes	cayenne pepper
2 shallots	boiled rice

Chop off the heads of the lobsters (a firm chop kills them at once; if you cannot face doing this, cook the lobster some other way – e.g. Newburg, see below – as this dish cannot be made with a cooked lobster). Remove the coral and keep it. Cut off the claws and break their shells. Heat the olive oil and butter together and, when they are very hot, put in the pieces of lobster. Cover and cook, shaking frequently, until the lobster is a good red colour. Drain off the oil and butter. Heat the brandy in a spoon, set fire to it and pour it, burning, over the lobster. Skin and *concassez* the tomatoes and add them with the shallots and garlic, finely chopped. Add the white wine and fish-stock, the chopped parsley and cayenne. Cook in a moderate oven (350° F., Reg. 4), covered, for ½ hr. Remove the lobster flesh from the pieces of shell and keep it hot. Reduce the cooking-liquor. Add the lobster coral and a little more butter to thicken the sauce. Arrange a circle of boiled rice (some use pilaf rice) round a dish. Put the lobster in the middle and pour the sauce over it.

Lobster Newburg

2 cooked lobsters of 1–1½ lb. each	1 glass Madeira
1 tablespoon butter	2 egg-yolks
salt and pepper	1 cup cream

Cut up the lobster in fairly small slices – including the claws. Toss them in butter. Season. Add the Madeira and cook slowly until it is almost absorbed. Keep hot in a *bain-marie*. Mix the egg-yolks and cream together and stir into the lobster – you cannot do this over direct heat as the sauce is liable to curdle. When the sauce thickens, serve at once. As in the preceding recipe, some boiled rice round the dish mops up the sauce.

Homard Thermidor

2 1–1½ lb. lobsters	1 glass white wine
1 tablespoon olive oil	½ cup fish-stock
salt and pepper	1 cup *sauce béchamel*
1 chopped shallot	1 teaspoon dry mustard
1 teaspoon chopped chervil and tarragon	E 2 oz., A 4 tablespoons butter
	grated Parmesan

Kill the lobsters by driving a knife into their heads. (I should not say this required practice; rather that you should have learnt from watching an expert before trying to do it yourself. As with *homard à l'américaine*, Thermidor must be done with a live lobster.) Cut them in half lengthways and break the claws. Season. Sprinkle them with olive oil and put in a moderate oven (350° F., Reg. 4) for 20 mins. Boil the shallot and herbs rapidly in the white wine and fish-stock to reduce by half. Strain and let it cool a little. Add the *béchamel* and mustard and bring to the boil. Add the butter to thicken. Keep the sauce hot. Remove the meat from the shells and claws and cut it up. Spoon a little of the sauce into the half-shells. Add the lobster flesh, then the rest of the sauce. Sprinkle on a little grated Parmesan and brown under a grill.

Homard au Whiskey

2 1–1½ lb. lobsters
1 tablespoon butter
2 tablespoons Irish whiskey

E ¼ pt double cream, **A** ½ cup heavy cream

Cut two cooked lobsters in half lengthways and cut the flesh in slices. Add the claws, cut up. Toss the lobster in butter over a low flame. Heat one tablespoonful of whiskey and set fire to it. Pour it, burning, over the lobster. Add the rest of the whiskey and cook till it is almost absorbed. Add the cream and heat till it bubbles. Fill the half-shells with the lobster and reheat for a few minutes in a hot oven.

Homard Archiduc

2 1–1½ lb. lobsters	salt and cayenne
1 tablespoon olive oil	**E** ¼ pt double cream, **A** ½ cup
1 tablespoon butter	heavy cream
2 tablespoons brandy	2 egg-yolks
2 glasses port	1 tablespoon butter
1 tablespoon whisky	lemon-juice

Cut up the lobsters and begin their cooking exactly as in
homard à l'américaine (p. 52). Cook till the lobster is a good red
colour, then drain off the butter and oil. Add the brandy,
burning. Let the lobster absorb it. Then add the port and the
whisky. Season. Cover and cook in a moderate oven (350° F.,
Reg. 4) for ½ hr. Take out the pieces of lobster. Remove the
flesh from the shell and keep it warm. Strain and reduce the
cooking-liquor. Add the cream and let it bubble. Bind the sauce
with the egg-yolks and finish with the butter and a squeeze of
lemon-juice. Pour the sauce over the lobster and serve at once.
Boiled rice will mop up the sauce.

Homard à la Crème

2 1–1½ lb. cooked lobsters	2 egg-yolks
E 2 tablespoons, **A** 3 tablespoons butter	**E** 2 tablespoons, **A** 3 tablespoons cream
salt, pepper and paprika	a dash of sherry or Madeira
1 tablespoon brandy	

Cut the lobster into fairly thin slices. Melt the butter over a low
flame and in it heat the pieces of lobster. It must not cook long
or the pieces will get hard. Season. Heat and set fire to the
brandy and pour it on. Beat the egg-yolks and cream together

with the sherry or Madeira. Mix this into the lobster over a low flame. Cook till the sauce thickens. Serve at once lest it should curdle.

If you like more sauce, use more cream and more sherry or Madeira. You will then need some boiled rice for mopping-up operations.

Barquettes de Homard Froides Matignon

8 **E** *courgettes* **A** *zucchini*	4 mushrooms
1 glass white wine	1–1½ lb. lobster (cooked)
1 onion, chopped	*fines herbes*
chopped parsley	*mayonnaise*
2 tomatoes	tomato ketchup
thyme, bayleaf	lettuce, hard-boiled eggs,
lemon-juice and olive oil	tomatoes
4 *fonds d'artichaut*	

Peel the **E** *courgettes* **A** *zucchini* and cut them in half lengthways. Scoop out the seeds. Cook them in an earthenware dish in the oven with the wine, chopped onion and tomatoes, parsley, thyme and bayleaf, a little lemon-juice and olive oil. When they are cooked, let them get cold. Chop half the lobster. Add to it the *fonds d'artichaut*, coarsely chopped, the mushrooms, *sautés* in butter, drained and chopped, the *fines herbes* and some *mayonnaise*, coloured with tomato ketchup. Fill the **E** *courgettes* **A** *zucchini* with this mixture. Slice the rest of the lobster thin and put slices on the **E** *courgettes* **A** *zucchini*. Cover with more tomato-ed *mayonnaise*. Decorate the dish with shredded lettuce, quartered hard-boiled eggs, and tomatoes, peeled and quartered.

From the Berkeley, Paris.

Crabmeat Newburg

As many crabs as you need to produce a pound of crabmeat – or buy fresh, but not frozen, crabmeat, if you can. Heat the crabmeat in butter, using as little butter as possible. Season. Add a glass of Madeira and cook till the Madeira is absorbed. When the crabmeat is heated through, transfer the pot to the top of a double-boiler or put it in a *bain-marie*. Beat two egg-yolks and a cup of cream together. Stir them into the crabmeat. Cook till the sauce thickens, but, if it thickens too much, stir in a little more cream and a dash of Madeira.*

  * Lately, a Lancashire friend to whom I had given this recipe got some fresh shrimps from Morecambe and made his cook apply the recipe to them. Yum, yum!

Meat

BEEF

Braised Beef

2 lb. rump	salt and pepper
flour	*bouquet garni*
1 tablespoon beef dripping	1 glass white wine
2 rashers of bacon	1 liqueur glass brandy
2 onions	1 cup veal-stock
1 carrot	button onions
1 turnip	baby carrots
½ head celery	baby turnips
1 leek	

Cut up the rashers and cook them gently in the dripping. Flour
the meat, add it and brown it on each side. Take it out. Chop
the onions, carrot, turnip, celery and leek and add them to the

bacon. Cook gently for 5–10 mins. Season. Add the *bouquet*. On this bed put the meat. Add the wine and the brandy. Cook fast to reduce. Add the stock (the quantity depends on the size of the braising-pan – the liquid should come to the top of the vegetable bed). Cover – with a cloth or paper and then the lid – and cook in a moderate oven (350° F., Reg. 4) for a good 3 hrs. After 2 hrs, see if it needs basting and thereafter baste every $\frac{1}{4}$ hr. When the meat is cooked, take it out and strain the sauce over it in a serving-dish. In theory, the beef should be served with the vegetables but, as they will have been reduced to a mush, it is better to cheat and cook separately as many button onions, baby carrots and turnips as you need, starting them in butter and adding stock. (If there are no baby carrots or turnips, use larger ones 'turned' and cook them longer.)

Bœuf Braisé Flamande

For this dish the beef is cooked as in the previous recipe and is served on a dish garnished with cabbage, carrots, turnips, potatoes, bacon and sausage.

Escoffier's way – and, indeed, Madame Saint-Ange's – is needlessly complicated. All I think you need is a small cabbage, cut in quarters, cooked in water or *consommé*, squeezed out and cut in halves or quarters again. The carrots should be tossed in butter and finished in stock. Likewise the turnips. The potatoes should be boiled and quartered (or served whole, if new). The bacon should be cut in squares, tossed in butter and drained. The sausage should be cooked according to its type – boiled or grilled – and cut in slices. The beef goes in the middle of the dish and the garnish is arranged nicely round.

Bœuf à la Bourguignonne

2 lb. **E** topside **A** top round	beef dripping
½ bottle Burgundy	flour
1 glass brandy	veal stock
1 onion	butter
bouquet garni	¼ lb. mushrooms
12 button onions	4 rashers of bacon

Have the piece of beef larded. Marinate it for 3 hrs in the Burgundy and brandy with the onion, sliced, and a *bouquet*. Heat some beef dripping in a *cocotte* and brown the piece of meat on all sides. Take out the meat and put it on a plate. Stir a little flour into the dripping to make a *roux*, cooking it gently so that it does not burn. Gently add some veal-stock and whisk well. Strain in the marinade. Season. Put back the piece of beef with any juice which may have run out of it. Add the *bouquet* and some mushroom parings. Add enough veal-stock to bring the liquid up to the top of the meat. Bring to the boil, cover and transfer to a slow oven (300–325° F., Reg. 1–2), where it should stay for 3 hrs. While the beef is cooking, prepare the *garniture*. The mushrooms should be *sautés* in butter and cut up in halves or quarters, according to size. The bacon should be cut in dice, blanched in boiling water, drained and tossed in butter. The button onions should be blanched, dried and *sautés* in butter. When the meat is two thirds cooked, take it out and put it in another *cocotte*, surrounded by the garnish. Skim the fat off the sauce, correct the seasoning and strain it on to the meat and its garnish. Cook gently for about another 40 mins. Transfer the meat to a serving-dish, surrounded by its garnish, pour over some of the sauce and serve the rest in a sauceboat.

A similar version of this dish may be done with the beef cut in large cubes, marinated as before and cooked with bacon, onion and mushrooms. The cooking time is then only about 2 hrs.

Beef Braised in Red Wine

2 lb. beef	chopped parsley and chives
flour	1 glass brandy
butter	*bouquet garni*
1 onion	2 cloves
1 leek	pepper and salt
2 carrots	½ bottle Burgundy
1 clove garlic	veal-stock

Cut the meat into large dice, discarding the fat. Flour them and brown them well in butter. Take them out and put them in a braising-pan. Chop the vegetables and cook them in butter till they are soft. Add the parsley and chives (and any other herbs you may have, except mint). Set the brandy alight and pour it over the beef. Add the cooked vegetables (with their butter). Add the *bouquet*, spice and seasoning. Add the Burgundy. If it is not enough to cover the meat, add either some more or some veal-stock. Cover tightly and cook for about 3 hrs.

Bœuf à la Mode

There are innumerable recipes for this dish but this is the simplest I know.

2 lb. beef	parsley
best dripping or pork fat	a *bouquet garni*
1 glass brandy	¼ bottle white wine
1 lb. carrots	salt and pepper
1 large onion	veal-stock
1 calf's foot	

Have the beef (preferably **E** topside **A** top round) larded. Brown it in a *cocotte* in the fat. Set fire to the brandy and pour it on. Add the onion and the carrots, sliced, and the calf's foot, blanched and cut in quarters; also the parsley, salt and pepper and *bouquet*. Add the white wine and cook briskly. Add enough veal-stock to come up to the top of the beef. When the liquid is boiling, seal hermetically and transfer the *cocotte* to the oven (280° F., Reg. 1). Do not look at it for 2 hrs. For the next hour baste frequently. For the last half-hour, leave the lid off.

Stewed Beef

2 lb. **E** topside **A** top round	beef-stock
3 onions	salt and pepper
1 tablespoon beef dripping	sugar
3 carrots	*bouquet garni*
2 tomatoes	¼ bottle red wine

Cut the meat into cubes, discarding the fat. Roll them in flour. Slice the onions and brown them in the dripping. Add the meat and brown. Slice the carrots, skin and chop the tomatoes, and add them. Add the seasoning, a generous pinch of sugar and the *bouquet* and cover with stock. Simmer. Add the wine and cook for about ¼ hr. Add more stock, if necessary. When very hot, transfer to a low oven (300° F., Reg. 1–2) and cook slowly for 2–3 hrs, looking from time to time to see if more (hot) stock is needed. If you like, you can parboil some potatoes, cut them in quarters and let them finish cooking in the stew.

Estouffade 1

<table>
<tr><td>2 lb. E topside A top round</td><td>1 clove</td></tr>
<tr><td>4 carrots</td><td>pinch of cinnamon and</td></tr>
<tr><td>4 onions</td><td> nutmeg</td></tr>
<tr><td>2 cloves garlic</td><td>bouquet garni</td></tr>
<tr><td>6 rashers of bacon</td><td>red wine and water</td></tr>
<tr><td>salt and pepper</td><td></td></tr>
</table>

Trim the fat off the beef. Cover the bottom of an earthenware pot with the rashers. Cut up the carrots, onion and garlic. Make a bed on the rashers of half these vegetables and on it put the beef. Cover with the rest of the vegetables. Add the seasoning, spices and *bouquet*. Then nearly fill up the pot with equal quantities of red wine and water. (It is important that the pot should be of the right size and not too big.) Cover with paper or foil and the pot's own lid and cook in a slow oven (300° F., Reg. 1–2) for 5–6 hrs. Before serving, remove the *bouquet* and skim off as much grease as you can. You can make it the day before you want it and reheat it – not too quickly.

Estouffade 2

<table>
<tr><td>2 lb. E topside A top round</td><td>½ bottle red wine</td></tr>
<tr><td>flour</td><td>1 cup beef- or veal-stock</td></tr>
<tr><td>2 onions</td><td>bouquet garni</td></tr>
<tr><td>butter</td><td>¼ lb. mushrooms</td></tr>
<tr><td>1 clove garlic</td><td></td></tr>
</table>

Cut the beef into fair-sized cubes, trimming off the fat, and roll them in flour. Cook the onions, chopped, in butter. Brown the pieces of meat with them. Add the clove of garlic, chopped, the wine, stock and *bouquet*. Cover and cook in a slow oven (300° F., Reg. 1–2) for 3 hrs. Slice the mushrooms and toss them in butter. When the meat is cooked, take the pieces out and put them in another pot. Add the sliced mushrooms. Strain on some of the cooking-liquor and simmer for ¼ hr.

Estouffade 3

Follow the previous recipe but substitute white wine for red. Instead of using mushrooms, use some tomatoes, skinned, squeezed out, quartered and tossed in butter, and some stoned black olives.

Carbonnades à la Flamande

2 lb. beef	**E** ½ pt, **A** 1¼ cups mild ale
salt and pepper	**E** ½ pt, **A** 1¼ cups beef-stock
beef dripping	1–1½ tablespoons brown *roux*
3 or 4 onions	**E** 1 dessertspoon, **A** 1
bouquet garni	tablespoon sugar

Trim the fat off the beef and cut it into thin and not very large slices. Season. Brown them quickly on both sides in dripping. Chop the onions and brown them. Take them out with a per-forated spoon (to drain off the dripping). Pour the dripping out of the saucepan and pour in the beer and the stock. Thicken with the *roux*. Add the sugar and boil the sauce. Put alternate layers of beef and onion into a pot (with a *bouquet* half-way up) and strain on the sauce. Cover and cook in a slow oven (300° F., Reg. 1–2) for 2–3 hrs.

Tournedos★ *Grillé Bordelaise*

Though doubtless a grill should be done under a grill, I find I make a better *tournedos grillé* in a very heavy frying-pan with butter or beef dripping (you can also use arachide oil, if you like and if you can get one that is absolutely tasteless). But however you grill your *tournedos* (**A** steak from small end of tenderloin), this is how you make a *sauce bordelaise* to go with it.

Sauce bordelaise

4 shallots	1 cup *demi-glace*
1 glass claret	1 tablespoon meat-glaze
pepper	squeeze of lemon-juice
thyme and bayleaf	1 tablespoon beef marrow

Mince the shallots and put them in a saucepan with the wine, pepper and herbs. Boil fast to reduce. Add the *demi-glace*. Simmer, skim and strain. Poach the marrow, cut up, in boiling water. Add the meat-glaze, a squeeze of lemon and the marrow to the sauce and, if you like, some chopped parsley. Serve in a sauceboat.

I like another piece of marrow – poached – sitting on the *tournedos*. Or you can have a *fond d'artichaut* on each *tournedos* and a piece of poached marrow in each *fond*.

Sauce bordelaise is equally good with a roast fillet of beef. You can have it, for that matter, with a grilled steak.

★ Steaks from small end of tenderloin.

Tournedos Mascotte

4 *tournedos*★
salt and pepper
butter
4 artichokes

8 new potatoes
1 truffle
1 glass white wine

Season the *tournedos* and cook them in butter in a heavy frying-pan. Parboil the artichokes, remove the leaves and chokes, cut the bottoms in quarters and toss them in butter. Cook the potatoes (they must be small) in butter. Slice the truffle and heat in butter. When the *tournedos* are cooked, put them in a dish with the vegetable garnish. Add the wine to the pan and cook to reduce. Strain over the *tournedos* and put the dish in a very hot oven for 2 mins.

Entrecôte Marchand de Vin

E 4 *entrecôtes*, **A** 4 rib steaks
butter
1 onion
4 shallots
¼ lb. mushrooms

¼ bottle Burgundy
salt and pepper
flour
1 marrow-bone

Peel and chop the onion and shallots finely and put them in a heavy saucepan with a little butter. Cook them till they brown. Slice the mushrooms and add them. Cook slowly with the lid on the pan, then take off the lid to let the liquid evaporate. Add the wine, season and cook, covered. Make a little *beurre manié* with butter and flour and add it gradually to the sauce to thicken it. Take the marrow out of the bone – don't use more than a tablespoonful or you will make the sauce greasy – cut it up and

★ Steaks from small end of tenderloin.

put it in the sauce. Put the pan in the oven so that the marrow melts. While this is happening, fry or grill the steaks. When they are done, serve with the sauce poured over them.

Entrecôte Beaujolaise

4 **E** *entrecôtes*, **A** rib steaks	4 shallots
olive oil	¼ bottle white Burgundy★
butter	salt and pepper

Cook the steaks in oil in a heavy frying-pan. Remove and keep hot. Pour away the oil and put some butter in the pan. In that cook the shallots, finely chopped, till they are pale golden. Add the wine and reduce by half. Season. Off the fire, stir in some pieces of butter to thicken the sauce. Pour the sauce over the steaks and serve.

Filet de Bœuf à la Noailles

2 lb. **E** fillet, **A** tenderlion	1 lb. onions
1 glass brandy	½ cup rice (cooked)
¼ bottle red wine	salt and pepper
butter	breadcrumbs

Get the butcher to lard the meat. Marinate it in the brandy and red wine for about 2 hrs, turning it over from time to time. Brown the meat in butter all round. Moisten with the marinade and put it in a medium oven (350° F., Reg. 4). Chop the onions finely and make them golden in butter. Put them and the rice in the dish with the meat, adding more of the marinade, if

★ It should, of course, be white Beaujolais but you probably will not have any, so a dry white Burgundy or a Muscadet will do perfectly well.

necessary. Cook until the meat is done (but still pink). Put the onions and rice through a sieve and then, with some of the cooking-liquor, into a saucepan and cook to reduce. Season. Cut the meat in slices, keeping it in its shape. Spoon some of the onion between each slice and spread the rest on top. Cover the whole with a thin layer of breadcrumbs, browned in butter. (Pour on, too, some of the butter.) Cook in a very hot oven (450–475°F., Reg. 7–8) for 5 mins.

The meat must be decidedly underdone when you first take it out as it will go on cooking while you are keeping it warm and will cook again in the final operation.

Ragoût de Bœuf Bordelaise

2 lb. **E** topside, **A** top round	4 rashers of bacon
1 glass claret	2 cups beef stock
1 bayleaf	*bouquet garni*
2 cloves	12 baby carrots
1 clove garlic	12 button onions
salt	12 baby turnips
8 peppercorns	12 button mushrooms

Cut the beef into cubes and marinate it in the wine with the herbs and seasoning. Cut up the rashers and put them in a heavy saucepan over a low flame to melt the fat. Take the pieces of beef out of the marinade and dry them. Turn up the heat under the bacon and brown the pieces of meat. In another pot, bring the marinade to the boil with the stock and *bouquet*. Put in the meat and bacon and cook briskly for 10 minutes, then simmer for ½ hr. Add the vegetables and cook in a moderate oven (350° F., Reg. 4) for about 1½ hrs. Remove the *bouquet* before serving. You can, if you like, add a small tin of *petits pois à la française* just before dishing up.

Steak Dumas

4 **E** fillet steaks, **A** steaks cut from
  thick end of tenderloin
salt and pepper
butter
marrow bones
E ¾ pt, **A** 2 cups dry white wine

E 2 tablespoons, **A** 3 tablespoons chopped shallots
E ¾ pt, **A** 2 cups reduced
  veal-stock
E ¼ lb., **A** ½ cup butter
parsley

Season the steaks and cook them in butter over a high flame.
Poach four pieces of marrow in boiling water. When the steaks
are done, take them out, put them on a serving dish with a piece
of marrow on each and keep them warm. Put the wine into the
pan and the shallots and cook to reduce by three-quarters. Add
the veal-stock and boil for a minute. Off the stove, add some
pieces of butter to enrich the sauce. Check the seasoning. Pour
the sauce over the steaks and sprinkle with chopped parsley.

Steak au Poivre

4 large slices of sirloin
salt
peppercorns
butter

olive oil
½ glass white wine
dash of brandy
1 cup reduced veal-stock

Trim the slices of meat, salt them, and press crushed peppercorns into both sides. *Sautez* them in a mixture of butter and
olive oil (more butter than oil) so that they brown on each side.
Remove them to a serving-dish. Add the wine, brandy and
stock to the pan. Reduce. Off the stove, add some butter. Pour
this sauce over the steaks.

Pièce de Bœuf en Chevreuil

2–3 lb. beef	$\frac{1}{2}$ bottle dry white wine
1 onion	$\frac{1}{2}$ cup olive oil
2 carrots	6 juniper berries
1 shallot	salt and pepper
2 cloves garlic	*beurre manié*

The best piece of beef for this is the so-called 'round', rolled and tied by the butcher. Have a dish or bowl only a little larger than the beef. Chop the onion, carrots, shallot and garlic and put half in the dish. On this put the meat, with the rest of the vegetables on top. Season. Add the wine and oil and leave in this marinade for 48 hrs, turning the meat over now and again. Towards the end of the marinating, add the juniper berries, crushed. Put the meat with the marinade in a *casserole*. Bring to the boil, then simmer, covered, for 3 hrs. Remove the meat, put it on a serving-dish and keep it hot. Put the vegetables and cooking-liquor through a fine mill. Reheat. Add a little *beurre manié* (flour worked into butter) and pour over the beef.

The dish is called ' *en chevreuil* ' because it is a method more frequently applied to venison. Vegetable *purées* go well with it: chestnut, celeriac, lentil, swede, etc.

New England Meat Loaf

FOR ABOUT 8 PEOPLE

2 lb. **E** fillet steak/**A** tenderloin	2 cloves garlic
$\frac{1}{2}$ lb. lean pork	3 stalks celery
$\frac{1}{2}$ lb. lean veal	$\frac{1}{2}$ lb. mushrooms
$\frac{1}{2}$ bottle red wine	$\frac{1}{4}$ cup grated Parmesan
2 bayleaves	1 bunch parsley, chopped

mignonette pepper	1 teaspoon salt
Worcestershire sauce	½ teaspoon chopped marjoram
1 cup breadcrumbs	3 hard-boiled eggs
1 egg	chili sauce
1 onion	bacon

Mince the meat and marinate it in the wine with the seasoning and herbs for at least 4 hrs, turning it over from time to time. Remove the bayleaves and chop the rest of the herbs. Stir in the breadcrumbs, the egg, lightly beaten, the onion, garlic and celery, finely chopped, and the mushrooms, sliced and *sautés* in butter. Add the Parmesan, parsley, salt and marjoram, and mix well together. Line a greased baking-tin the shape of a toast loaf with some of the mixture, leaving a trench down the middle in which you put the hard-boiled eggs. Cover with the rest of the mixture. Spread some chili sauce on the loaf. Cover it with rashers to prevent the top from getting hard. Start in an oven at 400° F., Reg. 7, and after 7 mins. reduce the heat to 350° F., Reg. 4. Cook for another hour. Turn out the loaf and serve it either hot or cold, cut in fairly thick slices.

VEAL

Côtes de Veau Basilic

E 4 veal cutlets, **A** 4 centre rib	butter
chops	basil
*¼ bottle white wine	

Chop some basil very finely and mix it into some butter. Fry the pieces of veal in butter, take them out and keep them warm.

* Or slightly less.

Add the wine to the pan and cook to reduce. Add some of the basiled butter to thicken the sauce. Pour it over the veal cutlets. This can equally well be done with *escalopes* of veal.

Côtes de Veau aux Fines Herbes

Follow the previous recipe but using a mixture of herbs: parsley, tarragon, chives, chervil, basil – but nothing as strong as sage.

Carré de Veau Poëlé au Chablis

E 2 lb. *carré* of veal, **A** centre rib	bayleaf
veal bones	2 cloves garlic
3 onions	veal-stock
4 carrots	salt and pepper
1 tomato	½ bottle Chablis
butter	button mushrooms
thyme	noodles

Cut up the veal bones, the onions, carrots and tomato, and toss them in butter in a *cocotte*. Add the herbs. On this bed, put the veal. Moisten with the stock and cook in a slow oven (300–325° F., Reg. 1–2), covered, for 2 hrs. Take off the lid and let it get brown, basting from time to time. Season with salt and pepper. Take out the veal and keep it warm. Put the *cocotte* on top of the fire, add the Chablis and cook to reduce. Strain the sauce into a sauceboat and serve it with the veal. Button mushrooms, cooked in cream, and noodles, cooked in salted water and drained, go very well with this dish.

Étuvée de Veau au Vin Rouge

2 lb. veal	1 bayleaf
butter	salt and pepper
½ bottle red wine	**E** 1 dessertspoon, **A** 1 table-
2 cloves garlic	spoon flour

Cut the veal into cubes and toss them in butter to brown them.
Add most of the wine, the garlic, bayleaf, salt and pepper.
Cover and cook in a moderate oven (350° F., Reg. 4) for 2 hrs.
Mix the flour with the rest of the wine and add it to thicken the
sauce. Cook for another ½ hr.

Veau Sauté Marengo

1 lb. lean veal	butter
salt and pepper	1 glass white wine
flour	1 cup veal-stock
olive oil	1 clove garlic
3 tomatoes	*croûtons*
8 button onions	parsley
8 mushrooms	

Cut the meat into cubes, season, flour them and *sautez* in olive
oil. Peel and *concassez* the tomatoes and add them. *Sautez* the
onions and mushrooms in butter. Add the wine and stock to
the veal and let it bubble for a few minutes. Add the onions and
mushrooms and the clove of garlic, whole. Cover and cook for
1½ hrs. If it is too runny, pour off the sauce and reduce it in
another saucepan, then pour it back over the veal. (You may
find it better to use less than a cup of veal-stock.) Put a few large
croûtons on the veal and sprinkle on some chopped parsley.
Serve in the dish in which you cooked it.

Escalopes de Veau au Vin Blanc

4 *escalopes*
salt and pepper

butter
½ glass white wine

Beat out the *escalopes* very thin. Season with salt and pepper. Heat some butter in a frying-pan and cook the *escalopes* on both sides. Take them out and keep them hot. If there is too much butter, pour some away. Put in the white wine to *déglacer* the pan. You must cook this for a minute or two so that the wine loses its raw taste and so that you can amalgamate the butter and the gravy which has oozed out of the veal into a sauce: this is best done by scratching at the pan with a metal spoon. Pour this sauce over the *escalopes*. If you have made too much, waste some of it: it is not pleasant to have the *escalopes* swimming in the sauce. Chopped or fried parsley looks nice, and a *purée* of potatoes mops up the sauce.

Escalope de Veau Chanticleer

4 *escalopes*
butter
¼ lb. mushrooms

2 port glasses Madeira
E ¼ pt double cream, **A** ½ cup heavy cream
½ cup *béchamel*

Have the *escalopes* cut very thin and beat them to make them thinner. Slice the mushrooms. Make a creamy *béchamel*. Heat the butter in a large frying-pan and cook the *escalopes* in it – they should take about 3 mins. on each side. Take them out and keep them warm. Add the mushrooms and cook till they are tender. If you have too much butter, pour some off. Add the Madeira and cook fast to reduce. Turn down the heat and add the cream and *béchamel*. Let the sauce bubble gently, then pour it over the *escalopes*.

Gourmandise Brillat-Savarin

4 pancakes	**E** 1 dessertspoon, **A** 1 table-
4 slices veal	spoon chopped shallot
butter	1 large glass sherry
¼ lb. mushrooms	Parmesan cheese

Make some pancakes – without sugar – 8 in. in diameter. Have
some fillet of veal cut in pieces about 1 in. thick and 3 in. across.
Chop the mushrooms finely. *Sautez* the pieces of veal in butter
and cook them till they are underdone, turning them over at
half-time. Take them out and keep them hot. *Sautez* the mushrooms and shallots in the same butter. Take them out and keep
them hot. *Déglacez* the pan with the sherry. Put a little mushroom and shallot on each pancake. On that put a piece of veal.
Season. On top of the veal put the rest of the mushroom and
shallot. Moisten with the butter and sherry from the pan. Fold
the pancake over to enclose the veal. Butter a fireproof dish and
in it put the packages. Put a lump of butter on each. Grate on
some Parmesan. Cook in a hot oven (400–430° F., Reg. 6) for
5 to 10 mins.

Foie de Veau au Vin Rouge

1 lb. calves' liver	salt and pepper
2 Spanish onions	1 glass Burgundy
butter	parsley
thyme, bayleaf, basil, parsley	

Chop the onions coarsely and *sautez* them in butter till they are
soft and golden. Add thyme, basil and parsley, finely chopped,

and a little bayleaf, crumbled. Season. Add the Burgundy and simmer for 5–10 mins. Meanwhile, cut the liver either in dice or in strips the size of whitebait. Add the liver to the *casserole* and let it cook through while the liquid just bubbles. Do not stir it or you may break the pieces. They should be cooked in 5–7 mins. They should be whole but not hard, soft but not mushy. Serve with *croûtons* of fried French bread on top and chopped parsley.

Fegato Col Vino Bianco

1 lb. calves' liver	butter and olive oil
flour, salt and pepper	1 glass sweet white wine

Have the liver cut thin by the butcher, then cut it in thin slices – about as big as sardines. Roll the pieces in flour, season and brown them all round in a mixture of butter and oil (not too much or the sauce will be greasy). Add the white wine and let the sauce bubble for 2 or 3 mins. Serve with *croûtons* and a *purée* of potatoes to mop up the juice.

Rognons de Veau à la Robert

4 veal kidneys	1 wine glass brandy
salt and pepper	1 spoonful made mustard
E 3–4 oz. A 6–8 tablespoons	½ lemon
butter	chopped parsley

If the kidneys are large, four would be too much for four people, so reduce the quantity to three. Remove fat and mem-

brane from the kidneys. Heat **E** 2–3 oz./**A** 4–6 tablespoonfuls
of the butter in a saucepan and in it put the kidneys, seasoned
with salt and pepper. Cook briskly for 2 or 3 mins. then cover
and transfer to the oven (400° F., Reg. 6) for another 10 mins.
Take out the kidneys. Add the brandy to the saucepan and put
it on a brisk flame. While the brandy reduces, cut the kidneys
into thin slices. Add the mustard, the rest of the butter, cut in
small pieces, the juice of about half a lemon and the chopped
parsley to the saucepan and mix them all well together to make
a nice sauce. Add the sliced kidney and any gravy which may
have drained from it to the saucepan. Let it bubble but not boil
and serve very hot.

Rognons de Veau Caroline

3 veal kidneys	salt and pepper
2 shallots	Dijon mustard
parsley	1 liqueur glass brandy
butter	½ glass dry white wine
1 clove garlic	

Remove fat and membrane and cut up the kidneys in slices
about ⅓ in. wide. Chop the shallots and parsley. Melt the butter
in a *casserole*. Add the shallots and the garlic (crushed but not
chopped). Add the pieces of kidney and the seasoning. Cook,
turning over from time to time, till the kidney colours. Heat
the brandy, set it alight and pour it on to the kidneys. Add the
wine. Cook fairly fast for 2 mins. Remove the garlic, sprinkle
with chopped parsley and serve as hot as can be. Plain boiled
potatoes, if you can get good ones, go well with this dish.
Although it is cooked with white wine, there is no reason why
you should not drink red wine with it – in fact I should prefer
to do so.

Rognons Sautés au Madère

4 veal kidneys	salt and pepper
½ Spanish onion	1 large glass Madeira
butter	chopped parsley
¼ lb. mushrooms	*croûtons*

Cut the fat off the kidneys, skin them, cut out the hard piece in the middle, wash and dry them and cut them in slices. Chop the onion finely and *sautez* it in butter. Slice the mushrooms and add them. Add the kidneys and some more butter. Season. Cook gently, shaking the pan, for 7 or 8 mins. Add the wine and simmer for 2 or 3 mins, just off the boil. Strain off the sauce and reduce it, keeping the kidneys warm. Pour the sauce back over the kidneys, sprinkle with chopped parsley and garnish with *croûtons* of bread, fried in butter.

The same process can be used with red or white wine instead of Madeira.

Rognons de Veau à la Liègeoise

4 veal kidneys	6 juniper berries
E ¼ lb., **A** 8 tablespoons butter	2–3 tablespoons veal gravy
1 large measure gin	

Trim the kidneys, leaving a thin layer of fat round them. Heat the butter in a *cocotte* and put in the kidneys. Cook them in a fairly hot oven (380° F., Reg. 5) for 30–40 mins., turning them over from time to time. Crush the juniper berries and add them to the *cocotte*. Heat the gin, set fire to it and pour it over the kidneys. Add the gravy. Cook them for another minute or two. Serve in the *cocotte*.

Ris de Veau Charentais

2 calves' sweetbreads	butter
lemon juice	4 slices bread
1 carrot	garlic
1 onion	6 shallots, chopped
thyme and bayleaf	6 mushrooms, sliced
salt and pepper	1 glass white port
1 glass white wine	2–3 tablespoons cream
water	

Wash the sweetbreads for 2 hrs in running cold water and then soak them for an hour in cold water with some lemon-juice in it. Make a *court-bouillon* with the carrot and onion, cut up, the herbs, seasoning, white wine and water. Bring it to the boil, let it get cold, then poach the sweetbreads in it and let them get cold in the *court-bouillon*. Take them out, dry them, cut them in slices and fry them in butter. Rub the slices of bread with garlic, fry them in butter and pile the sweetbreads on them. Cook the shallots and mushrooms in the same butter. Add the port and the cream. Cook for a couple of minutes and pour the sauce, unstrained, over the sweetbreads.

Moussaka

1 lb. veal	cinnamon and nutmeg
6 eggplants★	1 glass red wine
salt	olive oil
butter	breadcrumbs
1 onion	grated Parmesan
2 tomatoes	1 cup *béchamel*
chopped parsley	2 eggs
salt and pepper	
★ French '*aubergines*'.	

Slice the eggplants, sprinkle them with salt and leave them on a sieve or in a colander to drain. Chop the onion and *sautez* it in butter till golden. Peel and *concassez* the tomatoes and add them to the onion. Add the veal, finely minced, the parsley, seasoning and spices, and cook over a low flame. Add the wine and continue to cook. If the mixture is runny, turn up the heat to evaporate some of the liquid but stir all the time to prevent the meat sticking to the saucepan. Fry the slices of eggplant golden in olive oil. Cover the bottom of a buttered fireproof dish with some of the slices. Sprinkle on some breadcrumbs. Stir some breadcrumbs and some grated cheese into the meat and put it on the eggplant, then cover with the remaining slices. Beat the eggs and mix them with the *béchamel*. Pour this sauce on to the dish, sprinkle on some more grated cheese and breadcrumbs and put in a hot oven (400° F., Reg. 6–7), uncovered, for ½ hr to brown on top.

LAMB

Gigot de Sept Heures

1 leg of lamb	*bouquet garni*
salt and pepper	1 glass brandy
2 cloves garlic	water
butter	12 button onions
4 carrots	1 head celery
1 calf's foot	2 turnips

Bone (or have boned) a leg of lamb and lard it (or have it larded) with strips of salt pork. Chop the garlic and rub it and the salt and pepper into the meat. Brown the meat all round in butter, add the carrots, sliced, the calf's foot, cut up, the *bouquet*, brandy and some water. Cook, covered, in a slow oven (about 300° F., Reg. 2) for 7 hrs. (Look from time to time to see if it needs more water.) Brown the onions in butter, cut the best part of the celery into cubes and add it to the onion, add the turnip, cut in cubes or slices. Add them to the meat for the last hour of cooking. Put the *gigot* on a serving-dish, surround it with the vegetables and pour most of the cooking-liquor over it (throw away the *bouquet*).

Gigot d'Agneau Braisé

a leg of lamb	salt and pepper
pork fat	veal-stock
3 carrots	parsley, bayleaf, thyme
2 onions	3 cloves garlic
½ bottle dry white wine	

Heat the fat (or you can use oil) in a braising-pan. Brown the lamb all round and take it out. Chop the carrots and onions and cook them in the fat. Take them out. Pour off the fat, leaving the brown bits from the lamb. Add the wine and boil fast to reduce by half. Put back the lamb and the vegetables. Season. Add the herbs and garlic and enough stock to come two thirds up the joint. Bring to the boil. Cover tightly and put the pot in a slow oven (300° F., Reg. 2) for 3 hrs. Turn the joint over every ½ hr. Take out the joint and put it on a serving-dish. Bring the cooking-liquor to the boil on top of the stove and strain some of it over the joint.

Épaule d'Agneau Bonne Femme

a shoulder of lamb
garlic
pork fat
4 rashers of bacon
16 button onions
4 carrots

a *bouquet garni*
½ bottle white wine
1 cup veal-stock or water
salt and pepper
2 tomatoes

Bone the shoulder and stick slivers of garlic into it. Chop up the bones. Cut up the rashers, blanch them in boiling water, dry them and toss them in the fat. Take them out and drain them. Brown the onions in the fat. Take them out and drain them. Brown the shoulder all round. Pour off most of the fat. Put the pieces of bone round the meat, the bacon, onions, the carrots, cut up, and the *bouquet*. Season. Add the white wine and the stock or water and bring to the boil. Cover and simmer for 1½–2 hrs. Half-way through the cooking, add the tomatoes, peeled and quartered. Skim the fat off the top and serve.

Gigot Provençale

a leg of lamb
pickled pork
bread
milk
fines herbes
garlic
salt and pepper
1 egg
lard
1 onion
2 carrots

2 turnips
1 glass white wine
1 glass stock or water
bouquet garni
celery leaves
salt and pepper
3 eggplants
6 small onions
4 tomatoes
4 cloves garlic
thyme and fennel

Bone a leg of lamb and stuff it with a mixture of pickled pork, bread soaked in milk and squeezed out, *fines herbes*, chopped garlic, salt, pepper and an egg to bind the stuffing. Tie it up and brown it all round in lard with chopped onion, carrots and turnips. When it turns colour, add a large glass of white wine and as much white stock or water, together with a *bouquet*, some chopped celery leaves, salt and pepper. Cover and put it in a low oven (325° F., Reg. 2) for 2–2½ hrs. Peel the eggplants and slice them in rounds, salt them and put them to drain in a colander for an hour. Slice the small onions; peel, de-pip and chop the tomatoes; chop the garlic and fry them all in hot oil. Season. Add a little chopped thyme and fennel. Put the *gigot* on a serving dish, garnish with the fried vegetables and spread some of the vegetables it cooked with on top. Moisten with some of the cooking-liquor.

Salmis de Mouton

1 lb. lamb* (preferably shoulder)	⅓ pt water
4 lean rashers of bacon	1 lb. potatoes
10 small onions	salt and pepper
butter	a stick of celery
1 tablespoon flour	a head of garlic
½ bottle red wine	a *bouquet garni*

Cut the lamb into fairly large pieces, chop up the rashers and put them, together with the onions, into butter and cook till they all colour. Sprinkle on the flour and stir it in. Add the wine and water. Add the potatoes, peeled and cut up coarsely, salt and pepper, celery, *bouquet* and the garlic (not cut up). Bring to the boil and let it simmer for an hour. Remove the celery, *bouquet* and garlic and serve.

* Weight without bone.

Gigot en Chevreuil

a leg of lamb	butter
1 bottle red wine	flour
1 onion, sliced	1 tablespoon redcurrant jelly
12 peppercorns	salt and pepper
1 sprig bayleaves	nutmeg
olive oil	

Marinate the leg of lamb in the red wine with the onion, peppercorns and bayleaves and a tablespoonful of olive oil for 48 hrs, turning it over from time to time. Take it out and drain it. Roast it in the ordinary way with oil and butter, basting regularly. When it is done, take it out. Season with salt, pepper and nutmeg. Drain off the oil, leaving just the brown juice from the meat in the pan. Sprinkle in some flour to make a *roux*. Transfer this to a saucepan. Add some of the marinade and cook to reduce. Season. Add the redcurrant jelly. To make a very rich sauce, add, if you like, **E** ¼ pt/**A** ½ cup cream. Strain into a sauceboat. Serve the lamb with the sauce separately. A *purée* of chestnuts goes well with this.

PORK

Côtes de Porc à la Flamande

4 pork chops	salt and pepper
E 2 oz., **A** 4 tablespoons butter	cinnamon
2 cooking apples	1 glass Calvados

Season the chops with salt and pepper and brown them in butter in a *cocotte*. Take them out. Peel, core and slice the apples, toss them in the butter without browning them. Season and add a pinch of powdered cinnamon. Put the chops on the apple. Sprinkle on the Calvados. Put a tiny piece of butter on each chop. Put the lid on the *cocotte* and cook in a moderate oven (350°F., Reg. 4) for ½ hr. Serve in the *cocotte*.

Côtelettes de Porc à la Charcutière

4 pork chops	white stock
1 onion	salt and pepper
lard	French mustard
flour	gherkins
white wine	

As I look through the above list of ingredients, it strikes me, as it will doubtless strike the reader, as a somewhat vague recipe. Pray read on, undiscouraged.

Chop the onion and over a very gentle fire soften it, without colouring it, in as little fat (lard or pork fat) as possible. Sprinkle in some flour and stir with a wooden spoon to produce something not unlike a *roux*. Moisten with a little white wine and a little stock. Turn the heat up slightly so that the liquid reduces. Season with pepper – if the stock is salty, no salt is required. Keep the sauce bubbling, rather than boiling.

Season the chops with salt. Heat some fat in a frying-pan and put in the chops. Cook them about 5 mins. on each side to brown them. Turn down the heat and cook very gently for about another 10–15 mins.

Skim off any grease there may be on top of the sauce, which should be of the consistency of jam. Off the fire, add some

French mustard and a few gherkins – the vinegar washed off –
cut in slices. Reheat but do not boil.

Take out the chops with a draining-spoon to avoid having
any cooking fat with them. Put them on a hot plate and spoon
some of the sauce on to each.

Côtes de Porc à l'Auvergnate

4 pork chops	butter
½ white cabbage	fresh sage
I cup **E** double, **A** heavy cream	½ glass white wine
salt and pepper	Parmesan cheese

Cut up the cabbage (a whole one, if small) coarsely and cook it,
till it is done but not mushy, in salted water. Drain and dry it
very well. Put it back in the saucepan with the cream and seasoning and let it bubble for ¼ hr. Cook the chops on both sides in
butter and take them out. Add some chopped sage to the butter
and then the white wine. Cook to reduce slightly. Stir into the
cabbage. In a fireproof dish make a bed with half the cabbage.
Lay on the chops. Cover with the rest of the cabbage. Sprinkle
on some grated Parmesan and a little melted butter. Put the dish
in a moderate oven (350° F., Reg. 4) for 20–30 mins. Serve in
the same dish.

Saucisses au Vin Blanc

16 chipolata sausages	**E** I dessertspoon, **A** I table-
E 2 oz., **A** 4 tablespoons butter	spoon flour
I glass white wine	½ cup veal-stock
	lemon-juice

Blanch the sausages in boiling water. Prick them with a fork and fry them in butter, slowly, turning them round. Take them out and keep them warm. Pour away the butter from the pan, add the wine and let it reduce for a few minutes. Make a *roux* with butter and flour in another pan. Add the stock and bring it to simmering point. Stir in the reduced wine. Add a few drops of lemon-juice. Put the sausages either on to bread fried in butter or into a dish on which you have piped a border of mashed potato, and pour the sauce over them.

Côtes de Porc à la Dijonnaise

4 pork chops
E 2 oz., **A** 4 tablespoons butter
½ glass white wine
½ cup veal-stock
salt and pepper

½ cup cream
E 1 dessertspoon, **A** 1 tablespoon French mustard
parsley

Season the chops and fry them on both sides in butter. Take them out and keep them hot. Pour away most of the butter. Add the wine and reduce. Add the stock. Season. Stir in the cream and mustard. Heat but do not boil. Add, if you like, a few little bits of butter. Pour the sauce over the chops. Sprinkle on some finely chopped parsley.

Saupiquet de Jambon

One of the great restaurants of France is the Hôtel de la Gare at Montbard. I was given this recipe by the *chef* and *patron*, Monsieur Belin.

Soak a ham for 24 hrs. Cook it in water for 15 mins. per pound. Drain and put it in an oven dish on a bed of carrots and onions cooked in butter. Add a bottle of white Burgundy or Chablis, about twice as much white stock and a *bouquet garni*. Finish the cooking, take out the ham and keep it hot. Slice 1 lb. mushrooms and *sautez* them in butter. Add a spoonful of the ham's cooking liquor. Stir in a little *polenta* to thicken. Add about as much cream as wine and cook for about 15 mins. Finally, add a spoonful of *petits pois à la française* and a large glass of brandy, *marc* or Armagnac. Slice the ham thinly, pour the sauce over the slices and serve hot.

This can, of course, be done on a domestic scale, using just a few slices of the ham, making a much smaller quantity of the sauce and keeping the rest of the ham for the cold sideboard. I have even done it with a piece of gammon (boiling bacon).

Travellers' Pie

FOR 10–12 PEOPLE

¾ lb. lean veal	¼ bottle sherry
1 lb. pork (half lean, half fat)	slices of lean veal
¼ lb. ham	E gammon rashers, A slices of
1 onion, chopped	Canadian bacon
1 clove garlic, chopped	veal and bacon stock
chopped parsley	short pastry
salt, pepper and nutmeg	

Chop the veal, pork and ham and marinate them with the onion, garlic, parsley and seasoning in the sherry overnight. Line a pie-dish with slices of veal. Put in the mixture. Cover with rashers. Add some stock. Cover with short pastry and cook for 2–2½ hrs in a moderate oven (350° F., Reg. 4). Pour in (through a hole in the top) a little more stock and let the pie get cold.

Baked Pork with Wine and Oranges

FOR 6–8 PEOPLE

4 lb. leg or loin of pork, boned,
skinned, rolled and tied
E ¼ pt, **A** a good ½ cup clear meat
or chicken stock
garlic, parsley, marjoram,
rosemary, salt and pepper

E 4 tablespoons, **A** 6 tablespoons of Madeira, white
wine or dry Vermouth
breadcrumbs
3 oranges
a little olive oil

Chop a clove or two of garlic with a little parsley and marjoram, a scrap of rosemary, and salt and pepper. Rub this all over the meat, pressing it well in along the lean side of the joint. Pour 1 tablespoonful of olive oil into a baking-dish and put in the meat and all the bones and skin which have been removed. Let it cook for 10 to 15 mins. in a fairly hot oven (400° F., Reg. 6), before adding the hot broth. Then cook uncovered in a very slow oven (310° F., Reg. 2) for 2½–3 hrs. From time to time baste with a little of its own liquid. When the last ¼ hr of the cooking time has arrived, take out the bones and skin (they can be used again in a stock), squeeze the juice of half an orange over the meat, and add the wine. Strew breadcrumbs on the fat side of the joint and return it to the oven.

Slice the remaining 2½ oranges into thin rounds, and blanch them for about 3 mins. in boiling water to eliminate the bitter taste of the rind. Drain them carefully, and put them in the sauce round the meat for the last 5 mins. of cooking time.

Serve with the sliced oranges all round the meat and the sauce separately. This dish is even better cold than hot, and those who don't mind rather fat meat could economize by using boned and rolled fore-end of pork (**A** shoulder butt), which is quite appreciably cheaper than leg and loin.

I am indebted to Elizabeth David for this recipe.

Jambon à la Bragard

fresh cream	York ham
Gruyère cheese	nutmeg
8 small thin pancakes	Champagne

Take a fireproof dish large enough to hold four pancakes, the size of *blini* pancakes, without their overlapping. Cover the bottom of the dish with a thin layer of cream and sprinkle on some grated Gruyère. Put four pancakes in the dish. On each lay a very thin slice of Gruyère and on that a slice of York ham (without fat). Cover with the other pancakes. Pour on a little more cream and grate on a little more Gruyère. Grate on some nutmeg and put the dish in the oven. When it is brown on the top, sprinkle on a little Champagne.

This is first cousin – rather a rich cousin – of *croque Monsieur*, so should be served as a first course.

From Château de Saran, Épernay.

Fried Pork a Marinheira

1 lb. lean pork	1 onion
1 glass *vinho verde*	2 cloves garlic
6 peppercorns	2 tomatoes
paprika	salt and pepper
1 bayleaf	**E** 1 pt, **A** 2½ cups cooked
2 cloves garlic	cockles
2 cloves	chopped parsley
salt and pepper	1 lemon or 2 oranges
olive oil	

Cut the pork into 1-in. cubes and marinate them in the white wine with the spices and seasoning for 24 hrs. Chop the onion and garlic (the second lot) finely and gently brown them in olive oil. Add the tomatoes, skinned and chopped, and cook till they amalgamate with the onion and garlic as a thick sauce. If need be, thicken with a little flour. Season. Add the cockles and heat them, but do not boil them, in the sauce. Add the parsley. While the cockles are heating, take the pieces of meat out of the marinade and fry them golden brown in olive oil. Serve the pork and the cockles side by side in a dish and squeeze over them lemon or orange juice, as you prefer.

This is a Portuguese dish. The Portuguese do not, in fact, use cockles, but we do not have the proper shellfish, and cockles, I find, do very well.

Poultry and Game

CHICKEN

Poulet Étuvé au Champagne

1 roasting chicken
bacon fat
oil
12 button onions
½ glass *marc de Champagne*
½ glass brandy

½ bottle Champagne
salt and pepper
beurre manié
½ cup **E** double cream, **A**
   heavy cream
truffle

Cut the chicken in pieces and *sautez* them in the bacon fat and oil – do not use a strongly flavoured oil. When they begin to brown, add the onions. Heat and set fire to the *marc* and the brandy and add them. Add the Champagne. Season. Cover and put in a moderate oven (350° F., Reg. 4) for 20 mins. Take out the pieces of chicken, skin them and keep them warm. Strain the sauce into a saucepan and thicken it with the *beurre manié*.

Then add the cream and a little chopped truffle. Heat but do not boil. Pour this sauce over the pieces of chicken and simmer for a minute or two. You could serve the chicken surrounded by *créole* or plain boiled rice.

From Château de Saran, Épernay.

Poulet Sauté à la Crème

1 chicken
E 2 tablespoons, **A** 3 tablespoons butter
2 small onions
bouquet garni
salt
flour

1 tablespoon water
1 glass white wine
E ½ pt double cream, **A** 1 cup heavy cream
pepper

Joint the chicken, cut the onions in quarters, melt the butter in a heavy saucepan and add the pieces of chicken, the onions, the *bouquet* and some salt. Cook over a moderate fire, turning the pieces of chicken over, till they are nearly done. Then take out the onions and *bouquet*. Sprinkle on a very little flour and cook, uncovered, turning the pieces over, for another 10 mins. Add the wine and water and simmer. Then add the cream and let the sauce bubble but not boil. Grind on some pepper from a pepper-mill and serve.

Chicken Stanley

1 roasting chicken
4 or 5 onions
E ¼ lb., **A** ½ cup butter
1 glass white wine
salt and pepper

E 2 tablespoons double cream, **A** 3 tablespoons heavy cream
a pinch of curry powder (optional)

Brown the chicken all round in butter in a *cocotte* and take it out. Chop the onions finely and cook them till they are soft but not coloured. Put back the chicken, add the wine, season. Cover and cook in a moderate oven (350° F., Reg. 4) for about 1½ hrs, basting from time to time. Put the chicken on a serving-dish, spoon round it some of the onion and keep it hot. Strain the cooking liquor into a saucepan and cook fast to reduce. Add the cream and, if you like, a pinch of curry powder. Pour this sauce over the chicken.

Poulet Sauté

I shall give the basic recipe to begin with and then give some of the classical garnishes. A chicken which is to be *sauté* should be large enough to cut into two pieces of breast, two wings with a good piece of breast attached to each, and the legs, if you use them, divided in two – I prefer to be extravagant and use the legs for something else, for example cold or devilled for break-fast or luncheon. If you do use the legs, they require cooking longer than the breasts and wings. You should use butter or oil to *sauté* a chicken. If you use butter, you should clarify it first as ordinary butter tends to burn. If you use oil, do not use a strongly flavoured one: some people use a mixture of olive oil and *arachide*. I use butter, olive oil or a mixture of both. (Since writing this, I have taken to butter and *arachide*.)

Poulet Sauté Algérienne

Sautez the pieces of chicken. Take them out when they are done and keep them hot. Pour away most of the fat. Add a glass of white wine to the pan and let it reduce. Add some tomato, diced, a little finely chopped garlic and a spoonful of *demi-glace*.

Poulet Sauté Arlésienne

Sautez the pieces of chicken. Take them out when they are done and keep them hot. Pour away the fat and add a glass of white wine to the pan and some finely chopped garlic. Slice some eggplants and onions in rounds and fry them in oil. Peel and *concassez* some tomatoes and toss them in butter. Put the pieces of chicken on a serving-dish, strain the sauce over them, garnish with the eggplants and onion and put little heaps of tomatoes round the dish.

Poulet Sauté Bagatelle

Sautez pieces of chicken in clarified butter. Take the pieces out when they are cooked and add a large glass of Madeira to the pan. Let it reduce. Then add some cream. Pour this sauce over the chicken and decorate with asparagus tips and baby carrots, cooked in salted water, drained and sprinkled with melted butter.

Poulet Sauté Beaulieu

Sautez pieces of chicken in butter or oil. When they are cooked, take out the pieces and keep them warm. Add a glass of white wine and ½ cup veal-stock to the pan. Cook fast to reduce. Pour this sauce over the chicken and decorate the dish with artichoke hearts, tomatoes (peeled, quartered and tossed in butter), stoned black olives, and potatoes cut the shape of olives and roasted in butter (*pommes cocotte*).

Poulet Sauté Bergère

Sautez the chicken pieces in butter. Swill the pan with Madeira and veal-stock. Reduce. Add cream. Garnish with *sautés* mushrooms and straw potatoes.

Poulet Sauté Biarotte

Sautez pieces of chicken in oil. Swill the pan with white wine and tomato *purée* (preferably home-made, not out of a tin). Garnish with dice of fried eggplant, roundels of fried onion, *cèpes* tossed in oil, *noisette* potatoes, all seasoned with paprika.

Poulet Sauté Bonne Femme

Sautez the pieces of chicken in clarified butter. When they are done, take them out and keep them warm. Add a glass of white wine to the pan and a little thickened gravy. Dice some rashers of bacon and cook them with some button onions in butter. Turn some potatoes like olives and roast them in butter (*cocotte*) – or you can use small new potatoes, just boiled and tossed in butter, if they are in season. Put the pieces of chicken on a dish. Pour over the sauce. Arrange the garnish. Sprinkle with chopped parsley.

Poulet Sauté Bourguignonne

Sautez the chicken pieces in butter or oil. Swill out the pan with a glass of red wine. Add a spoonful of *demi-glace* and some finely chopped garlic. Garnish with glazed onions, diced bacon, mushrooms and chopped parsley.

Poulet Sauté Bordelaise

Sautez the chicken pieces. Take them out of the pan and keep them warm. Swill the pan with white wine, *demi-glace* and chopped shallots. Garnish with artichoke – bottoms cut in quarters, roundels of fried onion and *sautées* potatoes.

Poulet Sauté Cynthia

Sautez the pieces of chicken in clarified butter. Take out the pieces and keep them warm. Add a glass of Curaçao to the pan and set fire to it. Then add a glass of Champagne and a squeeze of lemon-juice. You should add a little chicken glaze but, if you do not have any, add a spoonful of chicken stock. Add some pieces of butter to thicken the sauce and pour it over the chicken. Garnish with oranges peeled (with a knife) and cut in quarters, and grapes peeled and de-pipped.

Poulet Sauté Escurial

Sautez the pieces of chicken in butter. Swill out the pan with white wine and *demi-glace*. Add diced ham and truffles to the sauce and some sliced mushrooms, tossed in butter and drained, and finally some stuffed olives. Pour this mixture over the chicken, arranged on a dish with a border of plain boiled rice. There should, in theory, be a fried egg as well per person – as in *Poulet Sauté Marengo* – but I think that is overdoing it.

Poulet Sauté à l'Estragon

Sautez the pieces of chicken in butter till they begin to colour. As they do so, take them out and keep them warm. Add a chopped onion to the pan and cook it till it gets soft. Stir in a little flour. Add a glass of white wine, $\frac{1}{2}$ cup of chicken-stock, made from the carcase, and a bunch of tarragon leaves (without the stalks), finely chopped. Season. Cook to reduce slightly. Return the pieces of chicken to the pan. Cover and cook gently for 20 mins. Remove the pieces of chicken and put them on a serving-dish. Cook the sauce fast for a few minutes to reduce it further and pour it over the chicken. Have a few extra leaves of tarragon, not chopped, which you have blanched in boiling water, and garnish each piece of chicken with one or two tarragon leaves.

Poulet Sauté aux Fines Herbes

Sautez the pieces of chicken in butter. Swill the pan with white wine, veal-stock and *demi-glace*. Add finely chopped shallots. Reduce. Add little pieces of butter, then chopped parsley, chervil and tarragon. Coat the chicken with this sauce.

Poulet Saute aux Huîtres

Sautez the pieces of chicken over a low flame so that they cook but do not colour. Take them out when they are done and add to the pan some white wine. Cook to reduce. Then add some oyster liquor. Stir in some thick cream and pour this sauce over the chicken. Garnish with poached oysters.

Poulet Sauté Marengo

After the Battle of Marengo, Napoleon's chef was distressed to find that he had practically nothing left to offer his master for dinner. From a neighbouring farmer he obtained chicken, tomatoes and eggs, from a neighbouring stream some crayfish, from a field some mushrooms. Nowadays we usually leave out the garnish of fried eggs and boiled crayfish but the rest of the recipe is as it has come down to us.

1 chicken	1 clove garlic
3 tablespoons olive oil	½ cup chicken stock
12 mushrooms	1 glass white wine
2 tomatoes	salt and pepper

Cut up the chicken and *sautez* the pieces in hot oil. Add the mushrooms and let them cook slowly with the lid on – the chicken takes longer than the mushrooms. When they are cooked, take them out and keep them warm. Add the white wine and reduce. Peel and *concassez* the tomatoes and add them together with the garlic, chopped, and the stock. Season. Cook to reduce. Pour this sauce – I don't strain it, but you can if you like – over the chicken and mushrooms. Sprinkle with chopped parsley and, if you like, garnish with *croûtons* of bread fried in olive oil.

Poulet Sauté Portugaise

Sautez the pieces of chicken in a mixture of butter and olive oil. When nearly done, add some onion and garlic, chopped finely, some tomato, diced, some sliced mushrooms and a generous glass of white wine. Cook this slowly on the top of the fire so that some of the liquor evaporates. Serve garnished with stuffed tomatoes.

Coq au Vin

1 roasting chicken	2 rashers of bacon
E 3 oz., **A** 6 tablespoons butter	salt and pepper
12 button onions	1 glass brandy
12 button mushrooms	¾ bottle red wine (preferably
1 clove garlic	Burgundy)
bouquet garni	

You can, I suppose, do this with a 'broiler', but personally I would never let a broiler darken my kitchen door. Although there are other tastes in the dish – onion, mushroom, garlic, herbs, bacon and, very important, the Burgundy – the dish is, after all, a chicken dish and should taste unmistakably of chicken. If you start with a bird which tastes of nothing, you will not achieve this.

Cut up the chicken, as in the directions for *poulet sauté* – wings, two pieces of breast, thighs and drumsticks. Cut the rashers into dice and toss them in butter in a *cocotte*. Add the pieces of chicken and brown them all round. Take out the chicken and put in the onions and mushrooms. Cook till the onions turn colour. Return the chicken, add the garlic, chopped, the *bouquet* and salt and pepper. Heat and set fire to the brandy and pour it over the chicken. Then add the Burgundy. Cover and cook for at least ½ hr. Remove the *bouquet* and serve garnished with slices of French bread, browned in the oven.

Poulet en Cocotte de Guyenne

1 chicken	salt and pepper
olive oil	2 or 3 carrots
12 button onions	4 tomatoes
3 rashers of bacon	1 glass Armagnac
a *bouquet garni*	1 bottle claret

Cut up the chicken as for *poulet sauté*. Heat the oil in a *cocotte* and put in the pieces of chicken. Then add the onions, the rashers, cut across, the salt and pepper and the *bouquet*. When the chicken colours, add the carrots, cut in slices, and the tomatoes, peeled and quartered. Set fire to the Armagnac and add it. Then add the bottle of claret. Cover the *cocotte* and let it cook over a low flame for at least 2 hrs. Correct the seasoning, if necessary, and serve in the *cocotte*. You may not need all the claret – it depends on the size of the chicken and the *cocotte*. It should be runny but not swimming. A *purée* of potatoes helps to mop up the juice.

GUINEA FOWL

Salmis de Pintadeau

1 guinea fowl	1 glass white wine
E ¼ pt, **A** ½ cup *demi-glace*	1 glass red wine
6 shallots	salt and pepper
thyme and bayleaf	*croûtons*
oil	

Roast the guinea fowl, keeping it pink, and cut it in pieces. Break up the carcase and pound it in a mortar with the *demi-glace*. Chop the shallots and cook them in oil in a heavy saucepan with the thyme and bayleaf till they are golden. Add the red and white wine, bring to the boil and then simmer. Add salt and pepper. Add the pounded carcase and the *demi-glace*. Cook for a few minutes, then strain through a fine strainer. (It is sometimes easier to strain through a coarse strainer first and then through a finer one.) Correct the seasoning. Pour this sauce over the pieces of guinea fowl. Garnish with *croûtons*.

Guinea fowl are not worth eating unless they are very young so you will not get enough for four out of one bird. These proportions are enough for two.

Note that *salmis* does not in France mean a clever way of using up remains: *salmis* on an English menu should usually be given a wide berth.

DUCK

Canard Grillé Chez Michel

FOR 2 PEOPLE

1 duck	1 glass red wine
butter	1 tablespoon veal-stock
2 carrots	½ glass port
2 button onions	**E** 1 dessertspoon, **A** 1 tablespoon *foie gras*
2 sticks celery	
salt and pepper	**E** 1 dessertspoon, **A** 1 tablespoon butter
quatre-épices	
1 glass dry white wine	French mustard
	breadcrumbs

This is a dish I learnt from Chez Michel, 10 rue Belzunce, Paris – two stars in Michelin and deserves them. It is difficult to do with an English duck as they seem to be bred in a different shape. It is essential to cut off the whole of the breast with the wing attached. The breast and wing provides, as it were, the main course; the leg, cooked quite differently, comes later with a clean plate and is, as it were, the savoury.

Having removed the breasts and legs, chop the carcase and toss it in butter with the carrots, onion, celery and seasoning. Add the white and red wine and the veal-stock. Cook for an hour and strain through a sieve. Reduce gently by half. Finish the sauce by mixing in the duck's liver, put through a sieve and mixed with *foie gras* and port, finally adding the butter in small pieces.

Now grill the wings, keeping them slightly pink on the inside. Put them on a serving-dish and cover them with the sauce. Serve with *une pomme golden* [sic], cooked brown in butter and cut in four.

Then comes the next course. Remove the sinews from the legs. Grill the legs and, when they are half done, spread French mustard generously on them, sprinkle lightly with breadcrumbs and finish the grilling. Serve at once, accompanied by crisp *pommes allumettes*.

Quatre-épices can be bought in shops that specialize in French spices – or, of course, at somewhere such as Hédiard, Place de la Madeleine.

Canard à la Mode

1 large Aylesbury duck	**E** ½ lb., **A** 1 cup butter
1 pig's trotter	8 button onions
1 calf's foot	6 baby carrots
4 carrots	a *bouquet garni*
4 turnips	1 glass brandy
2 leeks	½ bottle white wine

Blanch the pig's trotter and the calf's foot and cook them with carrots, turnips and leeks till the meat comes off the bone. Brown the duck in butter in a *casserole*. Brown the onions and carrots and add them to the duck with the *bouquet garni*. Heat the brandy, set fire to it and pour it over the duck. Add the white wine. Strain in the liquor from the trotter and calf's foot. Cook for 1½ hrs. Cut up the meat from the trotter and calf's foot and add it to the duck when it is cooked. (You may need only half.) Take out the duck and cut it up. Put the pieces in a *terrine* with the vegetables, pieces of trotter and calf's foot round them (discarding the *bouquet*). Skim the fat off the cooking liquor and pour it over the duck. Let it jellify. Serve cold.

PHEASANT

Faisan à la Normande

1 pheasant	2 glasses Calvados
butter	½ cup cream
4 dessert apples	salt and pepper

Brown the pheasant in butter on both sides in a *cocotte*, then put it in a moderate oven (350° F., Reg. 4) for ½ hr and baste regularly. Peel, core and slice the apples and toss them in butter – they should not be completely cooked. Take out the pheasant and make a bed of apple at the bottom of the *cocotte*. Put back the pheasant and put the rest of the apples round it. Heat and set fire to the Calvados and pour it over the pheasant. Pour the cream round the pheasant. Season. Cover the *cocotte* and put it back into the oven, turned down somewhat, for $\frac{1}{4}$ to $\frac{1}{2}$ hr.

Faisan en Casserole

1 pheasant	1 glass brandy
butter	1 tablespoon game gravy

Melt some butter in a *casserole* which has a lid and put in the pheasant. Cover and cook in a moderate oven (350° F., Reg. 4). Every 10 mins. or so sprinkle it with melted butter. When it is done – about an hour – take out the pheasant and keep it hot. Pour away some of the butter. Set fire to the brandy and add it and the gravy. Put back the pheasant and let the brandy cook for a couple of minutes. You should serve the pheasant in the *casserole* but, as it is extremely difficult to carve a bird in a *casserole*, it is really more practical to cut up the pheasant – 2 legs, 2 wings, 2 pieces of breast – and put the pieces back in the *casserole* long enough to heat through.

Salmis de Faisan

The recipe for *salmis de pintadeau* on p. 103 may be applied to pheasant, except that it is as well to use all red wine, rather than half red and half white. One pheasant should, of course, be enough for four.

WOODCOCK

I am not sure that I like the way woodcock is prepared in restaurants, with the insides mashed up and *flambés* with brandy. It is very hard to beat a straightforwardly roasted woodcock, but, if you want to gild the lily, set fire to a spoonful of brandy and pour it over the birds 5 mins. before they finish cooking.

VENISON

Venison Cutlets

Marinate the cutlets overnight in red wine with a tablespoonful of olive oil, garlic, parsley, onion and peppercorns. Take them out, dry them and cut off any bone or fat that has not previously been cut off. Cook them in butter over a fairly gentle fire so that they brown on both sides. (They must not be cut too thick or they will not cook through.) When they are done – as with steak, the length of time is very much a matter of taste – take them out and keep them warm. Pour away most of the butter. If any bits of brown from the meat are sticking to the pan, scratch them away to incorporate them in the sauce. Add **E** 2/**A** 3 tablespoonfuls of the wine from the marinade to the pan and the same amount of veal gravy. Let this cook for a minute or so, then pour it over the cutlets. A *purée* of lentils or chestnuts goes very well with venison.

Civet de Chevreuil

2 lb. venison (haunch for choice)	2 rashers of bacon
¾ bottle claret	4 shallots
onion and garlic	parsley and thyme
bouquet garni	salt and pepper
flour	1 glass Armagnac
pork fat	

Cut the venison into 1-in. cubes and marinate it in claret with onion, garlic and *bouquet* for several hours. Take out the meat, dry it and dust it with flour. Brown it in the pork fat and take it out. Cut up the bacon coarsely and the shallots finely and chop the onion and garlic. Brown them in the fat. Strain the claret from the marinade into a saucepan and boil to reduce. Put the pieces of venison back in the fat. Pour on the claret. Add the parsley and thyme, chopped. Season. Cook for a little while on top of the fire, then transfer to a slow oven (300–325° F., Reg. 1–2) and cook for about 3 hrs. A *civet* should really have its sauce thickened with the blood of the animal being cooked but you are unlikely to have the blood of your stag. If you happen to have the blood of a hare or even of a rabbit by you, you could use that; if not, want must be your master. But if you had any, this would be the time to add a tablespoonful or two.

I am in favour of letting the *civet* get cold at this stage and reheating it the next day but, if it suits you to have it now, here is the next operation.

Correct the seasoning. Heat and set fire to a glass of Armagnac and stir it in. Cook for another 10 mins. Serve with slices of French bread, browned in the oven.

Note: The recipe for *Pièce de Bœuf en Chevreuil* on p. 71, can, of course, be done with venison. Likewise that for *Gigot en chevreuil* on p. 85, though with this I should use only young roe-deer.

GROUSE

Grouse Grand'mère

FOR I PERSON

1 grouse	*croûtons*
½ glass brandy	4 mushrooms
game stock	

Melt some butter in a *cocotte* and put in the grouse. Put on the lid and put it into a fairly hot oven. Fry the *croûtons* (the size of ordinary dice) in butter and dry them. *Sautez* the mushrooms in butter and drain them. Baste the grouse with melted butter every 5 mins. They take rather longer to cook like this than in a roasting-tin, uncovered, so allow up to 40 mins. When they are done, take them out and keep them warm. Pour away as much of the butter as you can, keeping just the brown juices which have come out of the grouse. Set fire to the brandy and add it to the *cocotte*, also about a tablespoonful of game-stock (if you haven't got any, don't use a substitute). Cook for 2 or 3 mins. Garnish the grouse with the *croûtons* and mushrooms and pour the sauce over them.

Some think one grouse is enough for two. I don't.

PARTRIDGE

Perdreaux Flambés du Bocage

Lard and season the partridges and cook them in butter in a *casserole*. Take them out and keep them warm. Pour away most of the butter. Add a spoonful of Calvados and another of game-stock. Cut the bacon off the partridges and put them back in the *casserole* for a few minutes. Then put them on a serving-dish. Reduce the sauce and pour it over the partridges. Set fire to some more Calvados and pour it over the birds. Serve at once.

Perdreaux Bonne Maman

Stuff the partridges with a mixture of their own livers, *foie gras*, chopped parsley, chopped truffles and browned breadcrumbs. Partly cook them in butter in a *cocotte*. Then add a little finely chopped garlic, some slivers of truffle and a glass of brandy. Cover and seal the *cocotte* (with soft paste) and finish the cooking in the oven. Unseal and serve in the *cocotte*.

TEAL

Roast Teal

Clean out the inside of the teal well. Put back its liver with a lump of butter and a small bunch of parsley. Melt some butter in a baking-tin and put in the teal. Cook in a fairly hot oven (375–400° F., Reg. 5–6) – probably 30 mins., but it depends on their size. When done, take out the teal and keep them warm. Pour away the butter, just keeping the juices of the teal. Scrape the pan and add a glass of white wine. Stir the juices into it and reduce the wine. Pour this over the birds and serve them with bunches of watercress and pieces of lemon. Cayenne pepper goes well with them.

Some prefer red wine or port.

HARE

Civet de Lièvre

1 hare	1 onion
1 bottle claret	1 clove garlic
onion	flour
garlic	parsley, thyme, bayleaf
bouquet garni	2 lumps sugar
pork fat	salt and pepper
2 rashers of bacon	1 glass Armagnac
5 shallots	*croûtons*

Put a tablespoonful or two of claret in the hare's blood to prevent it coagulating. Make a marinade with the rest of the claret, onion, garlic and *bouquet*. Joint the hare and put the pieces in the marinade. Leave overnight. Take the pieces of hare out of the marinade and dry them. Flour them, brown them in the pork fat, then take them out. Cook the bacon, cut coarsely, the shallots, chopped finely, and the onion and garlic, chopped as you will, in the fat. Brown the hare's liver with them. Take it out and mash it up. Meanwhile you should have reduced the wine of the marinade by boiling it briskly. Put the pieces of hare back in the *casserole* with the bacon, etc. Add the herbs and sugar and the mashed-up liver. Bring to the boil and simmer either on top of the fire or in the oven for 2 hrs. Shortly before serving, stir in the hare's blood and the Armagnac and cook for at least 10 mins. more. Serve with *croûtons* of fried bread.

You can, if you like, cook some button onions and mushrooms separately and add them to the *civet* for the last 10 mins. of cooking. Some like cooked chestnuts in the *civet* but I prefer a *purée* of chestnuts *à part*.

Lepre alla Piedmontese

1 hare	butter
bayleaf	1 rasher of bacon, chopped
1 stick celery, chopped	1 onion, sliced
1 onion, sliced	1 teaspoon cocoa
8 peppercorns	1 pinch sugar
1 bottle red Chianti	1 glass brandy

Put some wine in the hare's blood to stop it coagulating. Joint the hare and put the pieces to marinate with the bayleaf, celery, onion and peppercorns in the wine. Keep it in a cool place, covered, for 48 hrs, turning the pieces over from time to time. Take out the pieces of hare and dry them. Melt the butter in a *casserole* and in it brown the rasher and the onion. Add the pieces of hare and brown them. Add the marinade and the blood and cook over a low flame for 2–3 hrs. When the hare is cooked, put the pieces on a serving-dish. Strain the sauce. Add the cocoa, sugar and brandy to it and reheat. Pour the sauce very hot over the pieces of hare.

Lièvre à la Royale

1 hare	6 slices raw gammon/ham
1 lb. pork (fat and lean)	onion and garlic
breadcrumbs	parsley, thyme, bay, basil, cloves
parsley	gravy or stock
1 clove garlic	½ bottle white wine
1 shallot	1 glass brandy
salt, pepper, nutmeg	
1 egg	

113

How this dish should be made excites almost as much argument as how to make a mint julep or a Lancashire hot-pot. However, at the risk of getting a lot of angry letters from readers who use other methods, here we go with mine.

Put some wine or vinegar in the hare's blood to prevent it coagulating. Chop the pork and mix it with the hare's liver. Soak the breadcrumbs in stock, squeeze them out and mix them in. Add the parsley, garlic and shallot, finely chopped, and the salt, pepper and nutmeg. Beat the egg well and mix it into the stuffing. Stuff the hare with this and sew it up. Line the bottom of a *poissonnière* or some such long dish with slices of gammon. Put the hare on this – on its back. Add the onion, cut up, 2 cloves of garlic, chopped, parsley, thyme and basil, chopped, a bayleaf, broken up, and 2 cloves. Add a soup-ladle of stock, the white wine and the brandy. Cook in a moderate oven (350° F., Reg. 4) for 2½–3 hrs, basting well. Take out the hare and cut the string, and put it on a serving dish, stomach side downwards. Skim and strain the cooking liquor into another pot. Reheat it. Thicken it with bits of butter or *beurre manié*. Add the hare's blood and let it cook for 5–10 mins. Strain the sauce on to the hare – or some on to the hare and the rest into a sauceboat.

Puddings

Apple Fort Belvedere

8 Cox's orange pippins	1 port-glass rum
E 1 tablespoon, **A** slightly over	1 tablespoon water
1 tablespoon brown sugar	

Peel, quarter and core the apples. Put them in a fireproof dish with the water and rum. Sprinkle the sugar over them. Cook in a moderate oven (350° F., Reg. 4) for ½ hr.

Baked Apple with Rum

Core some large cooking apples and make a shallow incision with a sharp knife round their equators. Soak some lumps of sugar in rum and put them where the cores were. Put the apples in a fireproof dish (not touching) and put a little water and rum into the dish. Bake in a moderate oven (350° F., Reg. 4) until they become fluffy round their equators – about ½ hr. Serve with a bowl of whipped cream.

Tarte de Solognote*

E 2 tablespoons, A 3 tablespoons butter
1 lb. cooking apples
E 4 tablespoons, A 6 tablespoons granulated sugar
puff pastry

In a round, flat fireproof dish put the butter, apples (peeled, cored and finely sliced) and sugar and cook till the fruit is well caramelized. Then cover the apple with a layer of puff pastry and cook in the oven for 10–15 mins. Turn upside down on to a large plate.

Pommes Lombardi

Peel, core and halve some medium-sized cooking apples and poach them very gently in syrup, and let them get cold. Make some *riz à l'Impératrice* (cream of rice). Whip some cream and flavour it with Maraschino (Cointreau would do, if you haven't any). Arrange the apples on the rice and decorate generously with whipped cream.

Instead of the whipped cream, you could make an apricot sauce, hot or cold, with apricot jam well laced with rum. This, however, is not Lombardi.

* This recipe seems to have crept in in error: there is no wine in it. However, it is so good I am going to leave it in. You could scatter a few drops of Calvados on the apple.

Pears in Red Wine

4 cooking apples	4 pears
water	¼ bottle red wine
cinnamon	½ cup granulated sugar
E 1 tablespoon, **A** 1½ tablespoons sugar	zest of lemon
	¼ cup chopped walnuts
E 1 dessertspoon, **A** 1 tablespoon butter	

Peel and core the apples and cook them in the oven with enough water to stop them sticking, a little cinnamon and the sugar. When they are done, make them into a *purée*. (You can, of course, do this on top of the fire, if you prefer.) Stir in the butter and let the *purée* get cold. Peel the pears, cut them in half and scoop out the cores and stalks. Make a syrup by boiling the red wine, sugar and grated (or finely chopped) zest of lemon together for 5 mins. Poach the pears in this, simmering them gently for 5–6 mins. (do not overcook). Take out the pears and let them get cold. Let the syrup get cold also. Arrange the pears on the apple *purée*. Pour over a little of the syrup. Mix the rest of the syrup with the chopped walnuts and serve in a sauceboat.

Poires Almina

4 pears	4 egg-yolks
sugar	2 leaves gelatine
water	**E** 1 pt double cream, **A** 2½ cups heavy cream
vanilla	
E ¾ pt, **A** 2 cups scalded milk	zest of orange
E 6 oz., **A** ¾ cup vanilla sugar★	1 glass Cointreau

★ i.e. sugar in which a vanilla pod has been stored.

117

Peel the pears and poach them in a little water with sugar and vanilla and let them get cold. Leave them whole or halve and core them, as you will. Make a *crème anglaise* (custard) with the milk, vanilla sugar and egg-yolks. Add the gelatine – off the fire. Strain and cool. Whip half the cream and add it. Put the mixture in an oiled *bavarois* mould in the refrigerator. Cut the zest of orange *julienne* and blanch it. Dry it and put it to macerate in the Cointreau. Whip the rest of the cream when you are ready to serve the dish and flavour it with the Cointreau in which the zest has been soaking. Turn out the *bavarois*, put the pears round it, decorate with the whipped cream and the zest of orange.

Pêches Cardinal

Make a syrup with sugar and water and a piece of vanilla pod. Skin as many peaches as you want by blanching them in boiling water (like tomatoes). Poach them in the just simmering syrup – they must be covered. A small peach will be cooked in about 4 mins.; a big one in about 6. Do not overcook them. Let them get cold, cut them in half and remove the stones. Take a good quantity of strawberries (discarding any of poor quality) and put them through a sieve or mill. Sprinkle some sugar on them. (Or you could reduce the syrup the peaches have cooked in and use some of that.) Skin some almonds and cut them in slices lengthways. The peaches and strawberries should be put on ice or in the refrigerator until you are ready to serve them. Then dispose the peaches on a plate or dish. Mix some Kirsch into the strawberry *purée* and spread it over the peaches. Scatter the almonds on top. It is subtler not to have cream with this dish.

'Peaches in Red Wine

1 or 2 peaches per person (the yellow-fleshed variety are especially good for this dish)

sugar
red wine

Approximate preparation time: 5 mins. for 2 peaches

Pour boiling water over the peaches, leave them a minute or two, then skin them. Slice them into a bowl or straight into wine goblets, strew them with sugar and fill up the goblets with an inexpensive red table wine.

Although one rarely sees this recipe in cookery books, it is a very typical and delicious French way of serving peaches.'

This comes to me by the kindness of Elizabeth David.

Pesche Ripiene

4 peaches
4 ratafia biscuits
candied peel

E 2 tablespoons, A 3 tablespoons granulated sugar
½ glass white wine
2 oz. almonds

Crumble the biscuits, chop a small piece of candied peel finely, skin and pound the almonds. Blanch and skin the peaches and cut them in half. Remove the stone. Scoop out some of the flesh and mix it with the biscuits, peel, almonds and a little sugar. Stuff the peaches with this, fitting the halves together so that they look whole. Put them in a fireproof dish. Mix the rest of the sugar with the wine and pour it over the peaches. Cook in a moderate oven (350° F., Reg. 4) for about 10 mins. Serve hot or cold.

Pêches Eugénie

4 ripe peaches
¼ lb. wild strawberries
1 liqueur glass Maraschino
sugar
4 egg-yolks

E 3 oz., **A** 2 tablespoons sugar,
   caster if possible (flavoured
   with vanilla)
¼ bottle Champagne
rose petals

Peel the peaches. Put them and the wild strawberries in a glass
dish. Sprinkle sugar and Maraschino on them and leave them
in the refrigerator for several hours. Beat the egg-yolks, add
the sugar and whisk them over a low flame. Add the Champagne gradually. As it thickens, put it in the top half of a double
boiler with hot, but not quite boiling, water in the bottom half.
Whisk until the sauce thickens. Then whisk on ice till the sauce
is quite cold. When ready to serve, pour this *sabayon* sauce over
the peaches and wild strawberries and scatter fresh rose petals
over the dish. (Do not use crystallized roses. The best rose for
the purpose is *Étoile de Hollande* as it is perfect for colour and
both smells and tastes good.)

    From Château de Saran, Épernay.

Raspberries

As a change from raspberries and cream, have sometimes raspberries with red wine, white wine or a liqueur. They must be
fresh and firm, not old and soggy – and it is impossible to use
frozen ones. Strawberries, being a much firmer fruit, take quite
well to being macerated in wine or a liqueur: it brings out their
own juice. But with raspberries it is best to sprinkle the sugar
and alcohol on them just before you serve them. Use caster or

E icing **A** confectioners' sugar. If you use a sweet wine, use less sugar than if you use a dry one. It is extravagant – but worth it now and again as a treat – to use the raspberry liqueur, Framboise. Use very little sugar: the liqueur is dry so you want to keep the whole dish slightly astringent.

Fraises à la Créole

Cut four slices of pineapple, removing the skin, and put them in the refrigerator. Take a pound (or slightly more) of strawberries and remove the stalks. Cut up an almost equal amount – slightly less – of pineapple into cubes and mix them with the strawberries. Sprinkle on some (caster) sugar and some Kirsch and let them macerate in the refrigerator for at least 2 hrs. Dish up the mixture on the slices of pineapple. No cream.

Fraises Empress

1 sponge cake
1½ lb. strawberries
1 glass Grand Marnier
1 cup Melba sauce
4 nectarines

about 2 dozen almonds
E ½ pt double cream, **A** 1¼ cups heavy cream
sauce sabayon

Cut off the top and bottom of a sponge cake. Cut it in pieces and line a glass bowl with it. Put in the strawberries. Sprinkle with Grand Marnier. Coat with Melba sauce (fine *purée* of raspberries). Peel and slice the nectarines and arrange them round the edge of the dish. Whip the cream and cover the strawberries with it. Blanch and skin the almonds and brown them slightly (under a grill or in the oven). Decorate the dish with the almonds. Serve a sauceboat of *sauce sabayon* separately.

I got this recipe from the Empress Restaurant, Berkeley Street, London.

Fraises Cardinal

1 lb. strawberries	2 oz. almonds
½ lb. raspberries	½ glass Champagne
sugar	

Take the stalks off the strawberries and put them in a glass dish. Sprinkle on some sugar and a little Champagne and put the dish in the refrigerator. Sprinkle some sugar over the raspberries and let them stand to bring out their juice. Then put them through a sieve (a mill does not get rid of the pips). Blanch and split the almonds. When ready to dish up, spread the raspberry *purée* over the strawberries and scatter on the almonds. Serve with (caster) sugar but not cream. (The classical *fraises Cardinal* does not include the Champagne but I think a touch improves it.)

Fraises Romanoff

Macerate some strawberries in orange-juice and Curaçao in a glass dish in the refrigerator. Whip some **E** double **A** heavy cream till it stands up but still remains light. Sprinkle in some caster or **E** icing **A** confectioners' sugar and a few drops of Curaçao. Pipe this *crème Chantilly* on to the strawberries.

Fraises Wilhelmine

Very similar to *fraises Romanoff* are *fraises Wilhelmine* but with Kirsch instead of Curaçao and, as it is not a sweet liqueur, a little sugar. Again, use orange-juice as well. Dish the strawberries up in a glass dish and serve a sauceboat or dish of *crème Chantilly*, flavoured with vanilla, separately.

Cerises Jubilé

Stone some morello cherries. Poach them in a little water with some sugar. Take them out when they are cooked and reduce the syrup. Thicken, if need be, with a little arrowroot. Make the syrup very hot and pour it over the cherries. Heat and set fire to a tablespoonful of Kirsch and pour it over them. Serve at once with lots of cream, whipped or Devonshire.

Brandied Cherries

Poach some cherries in syrup. When they are done, take them out. Add some brandy to the syrup (the quantity depends on the age of the company) and cook so as to reduce the syrup and take away the raw taste of the brandy. Pour the syrup over the cherries and let them get cold. Serve with vanilla ice-cream.

Cherries with Claret

Stone the cherries (morello are best). Put them in a saucepan. Sprinkle sugar on them and a pinch of cinnamon. Pour on enough claret to cover them. Cook them over a very low flame till they are soft. Let them cool in the syrup. Take out the cherries and put them in a glass dish. Reduce the syrup slightly and add a little redcurrant jelly to thicken it. Let it get cold and pour it over the cherries.

Plums Baked in Wine

1 lb. Victoria, Tsar or other good cooking plums
E 3 tablespoons, **A** 4½ tablespoons sugar
E 2 tablespoons, **A** 3 tablespoons each of port and water

The plums should be, preferably, slightly under-ripe. Wipe them with a soft cloth. With a fruit-knife make a slit in each plum, following the natural division of the fruit.

'In a baking-dish (I use a deepish oven-proof china bowl,' writes Elizabeth David, to whom I owe this recipe, 'but almost any baking dish will do provided it is not too large for the quantity of fruit, which should, if possible, be piled up rather than spread out in one layer) put the fruit, strewn with sugar, which can be brown, white or vanilla-flavoured. Alternatively a vanilla pod can be cooked with the fruit. Add the wine and water. Bake near the top of a slow oven (210° F., Reg. 2) for 35 to 40 mins. The timing depends upon the variety and relative ripeness of the fruit, which should be tender but still retain their shape. This dish is delicious hot or cold.

'Red table wine can be used instead of port. When no fresh plums are available, the same dish made with prunes is also very good. They need more wine and water, and much longer cooking, but no sugar.'

Prune Soufflé

1 lb. prunes
1 glass red wine
water

zest of lemon
4 eggs

Soak the prunes for 24 hrs. Put them in a saucepan with the red wine and just enough water to cover them. Add some pieces of zest of lemon. Cook slowly till the prunes are quite soft. Drain off the cooking-liquor, remove the lemon zest, stone the prunes and put them through a sieve. Moisten with a very little of the cooking-liquor, strained. Beat the yolks of the eggs and stir them into the *purée*. Whip the whites and fold them in. Put the mixture in a buttered *soufflé* dish and cook in a hot oven (400–425°F., Reg. 5–6) for 15–20 mins.

Prune Mousse

Soak and cook the prunes as in the preceding recipe. Dissolve a leaf of gelatine in the cooking-liquor and stir it into the prune *purée*. Whip some cream and add it to the prunes when they are cold. Put into a *soufflé* dish and leave it an hour or two in the refrigerator.

Prune Mould

Soak and cook the prunes as in the *soufflé* recipe but omit the red wine and use more water. Add the zest of lemon, as before, but this time add some granulated sugar. When the prunes are done, stone them and put them through a sieve. Return the *purée* to the cooking-liquor and reduce slightly. Add a glass of port. Test for sweetness and, if necessary, add more sugar. Dissolve a leaf or two of gelatine in the cooking-liquor and stir it in. Butter a mould and put in the mixture. Let it get cold. Put it in the refrigerator for 2 or 3 hrs. Turn it out on to a flat dish. Decorate with whipped cream or serve **E** double **A** heavy cream separately.

Stewed Prunes Boulestin

1 lb. prunes	½ vanilla pod
E ¼ lb., **A** ½ cup sugar	1 glass claret or port
E ½ pt, **A** 1¼ cups water	cream

Soak the prunes overnight. Drain them. Cook them over a slow fire with the sugar, water and vanilla pod. When they are nearly cooked, add the wine and simmer. Take out the vanilla pod. If the juice is too runny, take out the prunes, boil the juice to reduce, then pour it over the prunes. Serve hot or cold with lots of cream.

Figues Flambées

Peel the figs – they must be ripe. Prick them all over with a silver fork. Put them in a chafing dish and add a glass of liqueur for each fig. Set it alight. Turn the figs over so that they get cooked all round – or rather impregnated all round with the spirit. You can use brandy, Armagnac or *marc*; or brandy and Grand Marnier, mixed; or rum or Kirsch, according to your taste and what you have open.

Fraises des Bois

In my opinion, wild strawberries are much better with wine than with cream. Let each person serve him or herself and then offer sugar to all and a choice of cream or wine. I pour just a spoonful of the wine I am drinking over them.

Fruit Salad

The best fruit salads are made with fresh fruits in season. Apples, pears and bananas are a good basis. Peaches, nectarines and strawberries are good additions. A little orange is good but too much drowns the other fruit. So does too much pineapple. Cherries (which should be stoned) look good – don't use ones in syrup. A little mango is good. Pawpaw and melon in small quantities. Plums, currants, blackberries and gooseberries are not good in fruit salad. Cut all the fruit up (removing core, skin, stones, pips, etc.), keeping all the juice – do it over a bowl. Squeeze on a little lemon-juice. Add some zest of lemon and zest of orange, chopped finely. Sprinkle on a little (caster) sugar. Then sprinkle on some Maraschino or Kirsch and let the fruit macerate for several hours in the refrigerator.

Ananas au Kirsch

Anyone can make this dish. Give each guest a slice of pineapple (with the skin removed), pass the sugar (caster) and a bottle of Kirsch and let each person take as much as he or she wants.

Note: It cannot – well, it can, I suppose, but it should not – be done with tinned pineapple.

Ananas Créole

See *Fraises créole*, p. 121.

Melon au Porto

Cut a melon in half and scoop out the pips. Put a little port – do not overdo it – in each half. Put them on ice if you can – if not, in a very cold larder. It is better not to put them in a refrigerator as sometimes other things take on the flavour of the melon. If they are small melons, such as *Charentais*, serve a half to each person. If they are large, such as canteloupe, pour the port and juice into a sauceboat, cut the melon in slices and serve the juice separately.

You can do this with any kind of melon except a watermelon.

Melon aux Fraises des Bois

Cut a melon in half and scoop out the pips. Fill the hole with wild strawberries. Sprinkle on some sugar and then a little port or white wine. Leave in a cold place or on ice for a couple of hours. If the hole, especially in a *Charentais* melon, is too small, you may have to scoop out a little of the flesh to get the right ratio of strawberries to melon. Naturally, no cream.

Rum Omelette

Allow 2 eggs a head. Break them into a bowl and mix but do not beat. Add a pinch or two of sugar. Make an omelette pan very hot so that when you put a piece of butter in it melts at once (you need a teaspoonful for every two eggs). Pour in the eggs and keep them moving about with a fork. As they get solid, tip the pan away from you so that the omelette forms against the far side. With a palette knife, turn the half of the omelette nearer you on to the opposite half. Hold the pan with the handle away from you and bring the handle towards you so as to turn the omelette upside down on to a plate which you have made very hot. Sprinkle the omelette with sugar. In another saucepan you should have made some rum very hot. Set fire to it and pour it over the omelette. If you have two pairs of hands, one can burn the sugar under a salamander or grill while the other is heating and setting fire to the rum.

Plum Pudding

There are almost as many recipes for plum puddings as there are houses where it is eaten. I have given my inherited one else-where so give here one from Lady Harriet St Clair's *Dainty Dishes*.

'Four ounces of breadcrumbs (**A** 2 cups), two ounces of flour (**A** ½ cup), half a pound of muscatel raisins stoned (**A** 1½ cups), the same quantity of picked and washed currants (**A** 1¼ cups), a pound of sliced kidney suet, a quarter of a pound powdered sugar (**A** 1½ cups), a saltspoonful of salt, a little mixed spice, two ounces of candied lemon, orange or citron peel, chopped (**A** ⅓ cup); the rind of two and the juice of one lemon; beat six eggs well with some new milk, and a glassful of brandy. Mix all well together and let it stand two or three hours. Scald and flour a cloth, tie the pudding in firmly, and boil for five hours briskly. Serve with brandy butter and whipped cream.'

Brandy Butter

E 3 oz., **A** 6 tablespoons butter
E 3 oz., **A** 6 tablespoons sugar (caster)

E 3 tablespoons, **A** 4 tablespoons brandy

Work the butter to a cream and then beat in the sugar. Mix in the brandy gradually. Keep in a cold larder – it is liable to disintegrate in a refrigerator. If it does, add some more brandy and beat it all up again – you may need some more butter as well.

Mince Pies

Lady Sysonby in *Lady Sysonby's Cook Book* (1935) gave her great-grandmother's recipe for 'Minc'd Pyes'.

'Of apples, suet and currants, each 1 lb. (**A** 3 cups currants); raisins and sugar ½ lb. (**A** 1 cup sugar, 1½ cups raisins); candied orange and lemon of each 1½ oz. (**A** ¼ cup); ¼ oz. salt, of cinnamon and mace each 1½ oz. and ¼ oz. respectively; ¼ lb. Jordan almonds blanched and cut small; ¼ pt of red wine (**A** a good ½ cup); 1 glass French brandy; and mix all well together.'

This makes an excellent filling for mince pies. It is a matter of taste whether you have puff pastry or short pastry. If you like as little pastry as possible, have a mincemeat tart.

Trifle

Cut the top and bottom off a sponge cake, preferably a home-made one. Cut it in pieces and line a glass dish with it. Sprinkle it liberally with Madeira or a sweetish sherry. Cover it with a layer of raspberry jam. Cover that with ratafia biscuits or broken-up macaroons. Sprinkle them with more Madeira or sherry. Make a good custard (egg-yolks, sugar, creamy milk), and when it is cold, pour on a layer. Whip some cream, shaking in a few drops of Madeira or sherry when it has thickened, and spread on a layer of this. Blanch, skin and halve some almonds and stick them, point down, into the cream. Or you could decorate with crystallized violets or crystallized rose petals – but not, I hope, *glacé* cherries.

If you haven't Madeira or sweet sherry available, use port, Marsala or sweet muscatel. Some use rum but I don't like it. John Fothergill of the Spread Eagle, Thame, used to use the sweet Greek wine, mavrodaphne: I can think of no other good use for it.

Zabaglione

8 egg-yolks

4 half-shells sugar (caster)

4 half-shells Marsala

Whisk the egg-yolks and sugar together in a thick saucepan. Whisk in the Marsala. Put the saucepan in a *bain-marie* of not quite boiling water. Continue to whisk till the mixture gets frothy and rises. Pour into warmed glasses.

Nesselrode Pudding

20 chestnuts

E 1½ pts, **A** 4 cups water

E 11 oz., **A** 1½ cups sugar

vanilla pod

4 egg-yolks

E 1 pt double cream, **A** 2½ cups heavy cream

2 glasses Maraschino

E 2 oz., **A** ¼ cup raisins

Make a syrup with the water, **E** ½ lb. **A** 1 cup sugar and vanilla pod. Put the chestnuts in boiling water long enough to be able to take off their outer and inner skins – about 10 mins. Then simmer them in the syrup till they are soft – 30–40 mins. Put them through a mill. Reserve the syrup. Bring **E** ½ pt/**A** 1½ cups cream nearly to the boil. Beat **E** 2 oz./**A** 4 tablespoonfuls sugar into 2 of the egg-yolks and, over a very low flame or in a *bain-marie*, stir in the cream. Do not let it boil but cook it till it becomes a thick custard. Add the chestnut *purée* and one glass of Maraschino. Let it get cool, then put it in the refrigerator. Stone the raisins (if not bought already stoned) and simmer them in the syrup till they are quite soft. Take them out, drain them and let them get cold. Whip **E** ¼ pt/**A** ½ cup cream and mix it and the raisins into the chestnut *purée*. Butter a mould and fill it with this mixture. Put it on ice or in the coldest part of the refrigerator. Make another custard with the last of the cream, sugar and egg-yolks. It should thicken but not boil. Stir in a glass of Maraschino and let the custard get cold. Turn the mould out into a glass dish and pour the custard round it.

Pets de Nonnes

1 cup water	**E** 1 tablespoon, **A** 1½ table-
1 pinch salt	spoons sugar
1 coffeespoonful rum	**E** 2 tablespoons, **A** 3 table-
E 1 tablespoon, **A** 1½ tablespoons	spoons flour
butter	2 eggs

Bring the water to the boil. Add the salt and the rum. Add the butter and sugar and boil again. Shake in the (sifted) flour, whisking well. Cook till the mixture comes away from the sides of the saucepan. Take the saucepan off the fire and stir in the eggs, mixed but not beaten. Stir well as the mixture thickens. Heat some fat or oil (one without a strong taste) in a deep fryer. Drop in spoonfuls of the mixture and cook till golden. As they colour, take them out, drain them and keep them warm. Pile them up on a plate and sprinkle sugar (caster) on them. Serve with a hot apricot sauce to which you have added a few drops of rum.

Crêpes à la Crème

For the pancakes
E ¼ lb., A 1 cup flour
pinch salt
2 eggs
E ½ pt, A 1¼ cups milk

For serving
1 tablespoon Grand Marnier
1 tablespoon Cointreau

For the custard
E 1 pt, A 2½ cups vanilla-
flavoured milk
E 3 oz., A 6 tablespoons sugar
(caster)
4 egg-yolks

Make small, very thin pancakes in the ordinary way. Make a very thick custard. Spread some of it on each pancake, roll them up and put them in a tightly-fitting fireproof dish, Sprinkle sugar over them. Cook in a moderate oven (350° F.. Reg. 4) for about ¼ hr. Heat the Grand Marnier and Cointreau together. Take the pancakes out of the oven. Set fire to the liqueurs, pour them over the pancakes and serve at once.

This comes from Harry's Bar in Venice.

Crêpes Suzette

Opinions differ on the ingredients for the pancakes in *crêpes Suzette* but in my view it is up to the individual cook, provided they are small, light and thin. I would substitute sugar for the salt in the last recipe and add a dash of Grand Marnier to the batter. I advocate letting it stand for at least an hour before making the pancakes. The pancakes – unlike the English pancake which must come straight from the pan to the table – can be made well in advance.

Make some orange butter as follows:

3 lumps sugar	**E** 6 oz., **A** 12 tablespoons un-salted butter
2 oranges	
1 tablespoon granulated sugar	1 glass Grand Marnier

Rub the lumps of sugar against one of the oranges to get them impregnated with the flavour of the orange, and crush them with a rolling-pin. Peel the zest off the other orange and chop it finely. Squeeze and strain the juice of the oranges (though you may not need it all). Beat the butter to a cream. Mix in the sugar (including the granulated), the chopped zest, the Grand Marnier and as much orange-juice as the butter will absorb without losing its creamy consistency. Keep in a cold place until needed.

The final operation must be done in a chafing-dish. Melt some of the orange-butter and in it heat, one by one, the pancakes, turning them over at half-time. As they heat, fold them in half and in half again. Push them to the edge of the chafing-dish as each one is done. Add more butter, as necessary. When all the *crêpes* are heated and folded, rearrange them in the dish, sprinkle them with sugar. Pour some brandy and Grand Marnier into the dish. Heat it and then (cautiously) set fire to it. Spoon the burning liqueurs over the pancakes, shaking the dish from time to time. Serve when the flames die down.

Baked Bananas

4 bananas (8, if small)	rum
butter	brown sugar

Peel the bananas and cut them in half lengthways. Butter a fireproof dish. Put in the bananas. Moisten with rum and sprinkle some brown sugar over them. (Add a squeeze of lemon, if you like.) Bake in a moderate oven (350° F., Reg. 4) for 20–30 mins. Heat some more rum and, when you take the bananas out of the oven, set fire to it and pour it over them (or do this in the dining-room for greater effect). Serve with whipped cream.

Orange Cream

Peel the zest off an orange and cook it in very little water till it is quite soft. Pound it in a mortar. Add the juice of the orange, strained, a liqueur glass of brandy and enough sugar (caster) to sweeten well. Whisk in the yolks of four eggs. Heat **E** 1 pt/**A** 2½ cups of cream almost to boiling point. Off the fire, add the other ingredients. Whisk until it is cold. Pour into custard glasses and put them in the refrigerator.

Orange Jelly

½ oz. gelatine
E 1 gill, **A** a good ½ cup, i.e. 5 fl. oz. water
¾ lb. lump sugar

4 oranges
1 lemon
E ½ gill, **A** ¼ cup sherry
whipped cream

Wash and dry the oranges. Peel the zest off one of them and macerate it in sherry. Dissolve the gelatine in half the water. Strain it on to the sugar and add the rest of the water, boiling. When the sugar is dissolved, add the juice of the oranges and the lemon, strained. Strain in the sherry, leaving behind the zest. Turn into a mould (rinsed out with water and not dried) and leave it to set in a cold place. Turn out into a glass dish. Decorate with whipped cream into which you have mixed the zest of orange, finely chopped.

Compôte d'Oranges

Peel the oranges with a sharp knife so as to leave none of the pith. Cut out the pips, taking care not to include any of the skin which divides them. (This necessitates an in-and-out movement with a small, sharp knife.) Boil ¼ lb. lump sugar with **E** ½ pt/**A** 1¼ cups water to make a syrup. Add a bit of one of the orange liqueurs – Grand Marnier or Cointreau – a dash, if you like a dash, more, if you like to have a strong taste of liqueur. Put the oranges in this syrup and cook over a very low flame for about 5 mins. If the juice is too runny, take the pieces of orange out and boil the syrup to reduce. Pour it over the oranges and let them get cold. No cream – perhaps a sponge-finger.

Sack Cream

Heat **E** 1 pt of double cream/**A** 2½ cups of heavy cream, a well-beaten egg-yolk, ¾ glass of white wine, some sugar and a little chopped zest of lemon in a *bain-marie*. Whisk till it becomes quite thick. Take it off the fire and whisk till it is cold. Serve in custard glasses.

Sweet Avocado

2 avocado pears	1 glass sherry
E 2 tablespoons, A 3 tablespoons sugar (caster)	nutmeg

Cut the avocados in half, remove the stones and scoop out the flesh without breaking up the skin. Mash it up with the other ingredients and put it back in the skins. Serve very cold.

A Jamaican dish.

Soufflé Lapérouse

FOR 6 PEOPLE

E 6 oz., A 12 tablespoons sugar (caster)	6 eggs
E 2½ oz., A 10 tablespoons sifted flour	3 oz. *pralin*
	1 tablespoon rum
E ⅞ pt, A 2¼ cups milk	butter
E 2½ oz., A ⅓ cup crystallized fruit	sugar

Separate the yolks and whites. Mix the yolks with the sugar and flour. Boil the milk (it should have had a vanilla pod in it for the previous few hours) and pour it on to the egg mixture, whisking well over a low flame until it thickens. Chop the crystalized fruit finely and add it, the *pralin* and the rum. Beat the whites (with perhaps an extra one or even two). Butter the sides and bottom of a *soufflé* dish. Sprinkle them with caster sugar. Turn the mixture into the *soufflé* dish (it should come two thirds of the way up). Cook in a moderate oven (350° F., Reg. 4) for about 20 mins. Take it out and sprinkle sugar (caster) liberally on the top. Put it under a fierce grill for a few seconds to brown the sugar.

This recipe was given me by the great Restaurant Lapérouse, quai des Grands-Augustins, Paris.

Violet Soufflé

Make a white *roux* with 2 tablespoonfuls flour and 2 tablespoonfuls butter over a low flame. Whisk in 1 cup hot milk and whisk till it thickens. Let it cool. Add 2 tablespoonfuls granulated sugar and 1 of Kirsch. Add 3 egg-yolks, one at a time, whisking well. Whip the whites of 4 eggs and fold them in. Add ½ cup of crystallized violets, broken up but not pulverized. Butter and sugar a *soufflé* dish and turn in the mixture. Cook in a moderate oven (350° F., Reg. 4) for about 20 mins. When cooked, decorate the top with a wreath of crystallized violets.

I found this recipe in Alice B. Toklas' most amusing and instructive *Cook Book*.

I incline to adding a few drops of violet colouring – it is quite tasteless.

Chestnut Soufflé

E ¼ pt, **A** a good ½ cup vanilla-flavoured milk

E 3 oz., **A** 6 tablespoons vanilla-flavoured sugar (caster)

E 2 oz., **A** 4 tablespoons butter
½ lb. chestnuts
1 glass Maraschino
5 eggs

Slit the chestnuts and put them in boiling water for about 10 mins. Shell and skin them. Cook them in the milk with the sugar, Maraschino and butter till they are soft – about another ¼ hr. Put them through a mill with the cooking-liquor. Let the mixture cool. Add the egg-yolks, beaten. Whip the whites and fold them in. Butter and sugar a *soufflé* dish and fill it two thirds full with the mixture. Cook in a fairly hot oven (375–400° F., Reg. 5) for about 25 mins. Sprinkle **E** icing **A** confectioners' sugar on top and serve at once.

Orange Soufflé

E 2 oz., **A** 4 tablespoons butter
E 2 oz., **A** 4 tablespoons sugar (caster)
E 2 oz., **A** 8 tablespoons flour
E ⅓ pt, **A** a scant cup – about 7 oz. milk

1 orange
5 eggs
1 glass Curaçao

Cream the butter. Beat in the sugar and then the flour. Over a low flame add the milk gradually. Then turn up the flame and whisk well till the mixture has the consistency of very thick cream. Let it cool. Cut off the zest of the orange and chop about half of it very finely. Squeeze and strain the juice (you may not want to use all of it). Separate the whites and yolks of the eggs. Add the yolks, one by one, to the mixture, beating well. Add the zest of orange, the Curaçao and enough juice to give the mixture the right consistency – you mustn't make it too liquid. Whisk the whites and fold them in. Butter and sugar a *soufflé* dish and fill it three-quarters full with the mixture. Cook in a moderate oven (350° F., Reg. 4) for about 15 mins.

Clafouti aux Cerises

1 lb. sweet black cherries	½ cup vanilla-flavoured sugar
1 large glass brandy	**E** ½ pt, **A** 1¼ cups milk
½ cup flour	3 eggs
pinch of salt	icing-sugar

Stone the cherries and put them to macerate in the brandy for
a couple of hours. Sift the flour. Add to it the salt and half the
vanilla sugar. Mix but do not beat the eggs and stir them in.
Gradually whisk in the milk. Butter a fireproof dish and pour
in some of the batter. Cook it on top of the fire till it just begins
to solidify. Add the cherries (with not too much juice) and the
rest of the sugar. Cover with the rest of the batter and cook in
a moderate oven (350° F., Reg. 4) for about an hour. Sprinkle
some **E** icing **A** confectioners' sugar on it and let it cool a little.
(You can use less milk in the batter and substitute some of the
brandy and juice from the cherries, if you like.)

Clafouti aux Poires, Pruneaux, Pommes

You can make a *clafouti* with pears, plums or apples. In the case
of pears, you peel, core and slice them and macerate them in
Sauterne, brandy or Wilhelmine. Then use some of the juice
instead of the milk in the batter. Plums do well in one of the
plum liqueurs – Prunelle, Slivovicz, Mirabelle – the dry ones
calling for more sugar than the sweet ones. Apples call for
Calvados. But if you haven't any of these in stock, brandy or
Kirsch is perfectly adequate.

Rum Ice-cream

3 eggs
E 4 tablespoons, A 6 tablespoons
  sugar (caster)
E 1 pt, A 2½ cups milk

E 2 tablespoons, A 3 tablespoons dark Jamaica rum
E ½ pt double cream, A 1¼
  cups heavy cream

Beat the eggs and beat in the sugar. Warm the milk and pour it gradually over the eggs in a *bain-marie*. Whisk till the mixture thickens. Let it get cold. Add the cream and the rum and put it in an ice-cream freezer.

Savouries

It may have been noticed that I have not done a chapter on vegetables: there are so few vegetable dishes that require the use of wine, beer or spirits that it hardly seemed worth while. Similarly, I have not done one on eggs. I hesitated about doing one on savouries, but there are a few dishes I should like to put in somewhere, and here they are.

Welsh Rarebit

6 oz. English Cheddar cheese	Worcestershire sauce
1 wine-glass sherry	mustard
1 wine-glass beer	toast

Cut the cheese into very thin slices and put it in a chafing-dish or a heavy saucepan over a low flame. When it begins to melt, add the other ingredients. Stir with a wooden spoon. It should become stringy. Make a piece of hot toast for each person and spoon some Welsh rarebit on to each piece. Serve with mustard and cayenne pepper.

Fondue

I give a recipe for *fondue* on p. 16. Though the Swiss eat it as a first course, there is nothing to stop you having some on a piece of toast as a savoury: Swiss rarebit, perhaps.

Champignons Flambés

1½ lb. button mushrooms
E 2 oz., **A** 4 tablespoons butter
salt and pepper
E 2 tablespoons, **A** 3 tablespoons
chopped shallots
1 measure brandy
1 glass port
E 1 cup double cream, **A** 1¼ cups heavy cream
1 tablespoon *demi-glace*
fines herbes
hot buttered toast

Melt the butter. Add the mushrooms. Season. Add the shallots, previously *sautées* in butter. Heat the brandy, set fire to it and pour it over. Add the port and cook till the mushrooms are done and the sauce is somewhat reduced. Add the cream and the *demi-glace* and simmer without boiling. Correct the seasoning. Add the finely chopped herbs. Serve on toast.

Champignons Lapérouse

1 lb. button mushrooms	1 glass port
butter	1 cup cream
1 small truffle	1 cup *sauce hollandaise*
salt and pepper	Parmesan cheese

Cook some large button mushrooms gently in butter with a truffle, sliced *julienne*. Season. Add the port. Cook for a few minutes. Add the cream. Let it bubble but not boil. Put the mushrooms and sauce in a fireproof dish. Cover with a thin layer of warm *sauce hollandaise*. Sprinkle with Parmesan and brown under a grill.

Also, as might be guessed, from Lapérouse.

Potted Cheese

In the proportion of

3 lb. cheese	2 glasses sherry
E ½ lb., **A** 1 cup unsalted butter	½ oz. powdered mace

'Use Cheshire, Cheddar, Gloucester or North Wiltshire [what is that?] Pound the cheese and butter together in a mortar. Mix in the sherry gradually. Add the mace. Put into pots and cover with clarified butter.'

This recipe comes from the defunct Thatched House Club.

You can do the same with port and Stilton but I should leave out the mace. It is a good way of using up the end of a Stilton.

Fromage Maison, Relais de Parme

1 Camembert
the same amount of Brie
2 *chèvres*
¼ lb. Roquefort
E ½ pt double cream, **A** 1¼ cups
  heavy cream

E 3–4 oz., **A** 6–8 tablespoons
  butter
12 walnuts
salt and pepper
1 large glass Armagnac

Cut the outside off the *chèvres* (goat cheeses). Shell, blanch and peel the walnuts and chop them up. Mix all the ingredients together – in a blender, if you have one – and put in a glass dish.

I got this recipe from Monsieur Laporte who runs that marvellous restaurant, the Relais de Parme, at Biarritz Airport. They make it every day. The quantities would have to be adjusted for a small household though this amount would be fine for a large buffet luncheon.

Some Drinks

After those 146 pages of serious writing about food, perhaps we need a drink – or at least a not very serious chapter about drinks – drinks made with wine and with other kinds of alcohol. It is not intended to be a definitive study of punches, neguses, toddies, mulls and cups. It is just a random collection of drinks that may be considered fun to have now and again. Here are some German *Bowlen* or cups to begin with.

Peach Cup

Cut some peaches in half, without peeling them, and throw away the stones. Slice them and put them in a glass bowl on ice. Sprinkle sugar on them and let them stand for 3 hrs. Pour a chilled bottle of Moselle over them and let them stand for another hour. Immediately before serving, pour another bottle of Moselle over them – it must be very cold – and an equally cold bottle of Champagne. Add a little more sugar, if you like – I shouldn't – and serve at once.

Strawberry Cup

Remove the stalks from some strawberries and cut them in half – or, if very large, in quarters. Sprinkle sugar on them and leave them for an hour or two in the refrigerator. Pour a bottle of chilled Moselle over them and leave for another hour. Just before serving, add a bottle of Champagne.

Cucumber Cup

Slice a cucumber, leaving the skin on. Pour a bottle of light red wine over it – it should be German wine but, as that is rare in England, use a Bourgeuil, if you can get one. A light Italian wine would do. Put the bowl in the coldest part of the refrigerator or on ice and let it stand for ½ hr. Add a bottle of very cold Champagne.

Mai Bowle

This is the most wonderful German spring drink, the May bowl, the Waldmeister Bowle or Woodruff Cup. May is the season of wild woodruff – *asperula odorata* – which beats even

borage as a flavourer of wine cups. The flavour is very power-
ful, and it must not be left too long in the wine – a splendid
excuse for frequent tasting.

Put a bottle – or some bottles, according to how much you
need – of fairly dry Palatinate wine in a bowl. Throw in some
woodruff – quite a lot. Taste frequently to make sure the woodruff does not eclipse the wine. As soon as you think the wine
has taken on enough of the woodruff flavour, take it out. Keep
the wine very cold. When ready to serve, add cold Champagne
in the proportion of one bottle to every bottle of still wine.

Kalte Ente

Literally 'cold duck' – don't ask me why.

Peel the zest off a lemon, if possible in a long piece as one
peels an apple. Put some chilled wine – Moselle, Palatinate or
Rhinehesse, not too sweet but not acid – in a bowl. Add the
lemon and leave it till it has transferred its flavour to the wine –
but it must not be so lemony as to kill the wine. Here, again,
frequent tasting is necessary. Take the lemon out. Sweeten, if
you think it necessary, with a dash of Gomme syrup – I should
not. When ready to serve, add bottle for bottle of iced Champagne. For a teenage party, it might be prudent to add also a
certain amount of iced soda water.

Kullerpfirsiche

Spinning peaches.

For each person you need a large goblet, capable of holding
a peach and half a bottle of Champagne – a finger-bowl would

do. Give each guest an unpeeled peach and a half-bottle of chilled Champagne. They must prick their peaches all over with a silver fork and then put them in their goblets. Then they must add the Champagne. The effect of the Champagne on the perforated peaches is to make them whizz round. You drink the Champagne and subsequently eat the peaches.

Finally a recipe which I have never had the courage to try:

Kaiserpunsch

Make a sort of fruit salad of pineapple and orange with rather less apple and banana. Pour over it a bottle of Rhine wine and let it stand an hour. Before serving, add a bottle of Champagne and a bottle of arrack. 'Everything', the author says, 'must be very cold or it is impossible to drink this lethal stuff – but it tastes really good.' I accept no responsibility for the effects of this crazy recipe.

End of the German section, but, while on the subject of Champagne drinks, I must include some of my favourites.

Buck's Fizz

Champagne-orange, in France.

Shake some fresh orange juice on ice. Pour into a glass and add an equal quantity of Champagne.

Bellini

Shake some fresh peach juice on ice. Pour into a glass and add an equal quantity of Champagne. Asti Spumante can be substituted for Champagne. Tinned peaches cannot be substituted for fresh ones, though Italian or South African peaches are just as good for the purpose as English hothouse peaches and a good deal less expensive.

From Harry's Bar in Venice.

Tiziano

When fresh peaches run out, they stop making Bellinis in Harry's Bar and use grape-juice to make a Tiziano. Not as good.

Rajah's Punch

Very cold Champagne, laced with brandy – absolutely lethal.

Cup Royal

1 bottle of brandy	2 bottles Champagne
1 bottle Curaçao	fruit, borage, cucumber peel
2 bottles claret	

Macerate the fruit – strawberries, raspberries, grapes, peaches, nectarines, zest of orange and lemon – with the borage and cucumber peel in the brandy, Curaçao and claret all day on ice. When the guests arrive, add the Champagne, well iced. Carriages and ambulances at midnight.

A Summer Cup

2 bottles Moselle
1 bottle Champagne
12 strawberries
1 peach, skinned and sliced
a little cucumber peel
borage

Macerate the strawberries, peach, cucumber peel and borage in the Moselle in jugs on ice. Put the Champagne on ice. Add the Champagne to the jugs just before serving.

Planter's Punch

crushed ice
1 measure fresh lime-juice
1 measure syrup (home-made or Gomme)
2 measures not-too-sweet rum
Angostura bitters
soda water
nutmeg

Fill a half-pint glass three-quarters full of crushed ice. Add the juice of a fresh lime (lemon-juice will do if you have no limes) and the syrup. Add the rum. Sprinkle on a few drops of Angostura. Add a splash of soda. Grate on a little nutmeg. Drink through a straw.

From The Inn, English Harbour, Antigua.

Sangria

1 orange	1 liqueur glass Grand Marnier
1 lemon	(optional)
1 bottle red Rioja	2 splashes of soda-water
2 liqueur glasses Spanish brandy	

Put some pieces of ice in a jug. Peel the orange and lemon without breaking the peel and so that all the pith comes off. Hang them on the edge of the jug so that the peel drapes down inside. Put in the peeled orange and lemon and poke them with a wooden spoon to extract some of the juice. Add the wine, brandy and, if used, the Grand Marnier and stir. Take out the ice to avoid diluting the drink. Add a dash of soda-water just before serving.

Norman Douglas's Aphrodisiac Drink

Put together in a glass: two lumps of sugar and eight drops of Curaçao. Fill up the glass with port. Pour it in a receptacle and boil it. When just boiling take it off the fire and serve hot with a slice of lemon and nutmeg sprinkled over it.

Mulled Burgundy

Take a goodish bottle of Burgundy – not a Richebourg but, on the other hand, not Big Tree. To every bottle add a tot of brandy and a tot of apricot brandy, two or three lumps of sugar, two or three cloves, a tiny piece of cinnamon and a little lemon-zest. Bring almost to the boil and strain into glasses.

Philadelphia Apple Toddy

Bake 12 dessert apples without peeling or coring them. Put them in a large jug with 2 bottles of Jamaica rum, 1 bottle brandy, 12 lumps sugar, 2 qts boiling water. Cover and put in a *bain-marie* to infuse for 2 hrs. Stir from time to time.

Glasgow Het Pint

Grate a nutmeg into **E** 2 qts/**A** 5 pts of mild ale and bring to boiling point. Mix a little cold ale with sugar and gradually add two egg-yolks, well beaten. Ladle out slowly into the hot ale, taking care that the mixture does not curdle. Put in **E** ½ pt/**A** 1¼ cups of whisky or rum and return the mixture to the saucepan. Stir till it reaches boiling point, and then briskly pour it from one vessel to another till it becomes smooth and bright.

From Mistress Meg Dods.

Bishop

Make several incisions in the rind of a lemon. Stick cloves in these and roast the lemon by a slow fire. Put small but equal quantities of cloves, mace and allspice with a race of ginger into a saucepan with ½ pt of water. Let it boil until it is reduced one half. Boil one bottle of port wine, burn a portion of the spirit out of it by applying a lighted paper to the saucepan. Put the roasted lemon and spice into the wine, stir it up well, and let it stand near the fire for 10 mins. Rub a few knobs of sugar on the rind of lemon, put the sugar into a bowl or jug, with the juice of half a lemon (not roasted), pour the wine into it, grate in some nutmeg, sweeten it to your taste and serve with lemon and spice floating in it.

From Eliza Acton.

Hot Toddy

'2 jiggers Calvados   1 jigger apricot brandy

Warm over the flame. Slowly pour in a jigger of cream. Do not stir.*'

From Alice B. Toklas and attributed to Flaubert.

* All too likely you won't be able to.

Glossary

ASPIC: clear, savoury jelly, made of stock.

BAIN-MARIE: a receptacle, filled with hot water, in which one or more smaller utensils can be kept hot.

BEURRE MANIÉ: butter and flour, mixed together (4 oz. butter to 3 oz. flour) and used for thickening.

BLANCHING: preliminary cooking in boiling water – often done to remove skins.

BOUILLON: stock or broth.

BOUQUET GARNI: a bundle of herbs, tied together – usually parsley, bayleaf and thyme.

BRAISING: cooking first on top of the fire and then in the oven.

CARAMEL: sugar and water, cooked to a brown syrup.

CASSEROLE: metal or earthenware utensil for cooking on top of the stove and in the oven

CISELER: of vegetables, to cut finer than *julienne* (*q.v.*).

CLARIFY: to make clear, as of *consommé*.

COCOTTE: similar to *casserole*.

CONCASSER: to chop roughly.

COURT-BOUILLON: water, flavoured with herbs, for cooking fish.

CROÛTONS: pieces of bread, fried in butter – in dice for soups, in large diamonds and other shapes for garnishing meat or egg dishes – where appropriate, fried in oil. I prefer the old English word 'sippets'.

DEMI-GLACE: much-reduced brown sauce.

FARCE: stuffing, forcemeat.

FLAKE: to break into pieces with a fork (usually of fish).

FUMET: essence extracted from fish or game.

GOUJONS: sole, cut like whitebait.

GRATINER: to make a crust on top (in the oven or under a grill).

INCISER: to score or make cuts about an inch apart on the skin (ordinarily, of a fish).

JULIENNE: cut thin, like matchsticks.

KNEAD: mix with the hands, applying pressure.

LIAISON: a mixture for binding ingredients together, particularly egg-yolk and cream in thick soup.

MACERATE: similar to marinate (below) but with fruit.

MAÎTRE D'HÔTEL BUTTER: butter with parsley, salt, pepper and lemon-juice creamed into it.

MANIÉ: see BEURRE MANIÉ.

MARINADE: a liquid, seasoned and spiced, in which fish or meat is soaked before cooking. *Verb:* to marinate.

MIGNONETTE PEPPER: peppercorns pounded.

MILL: a device for making *purées*.

MOLLET: (of eggs) boiled for five minutes and shelled.

PIECE OF LEMON: a half or quarter of a lemon, large enough to be squeezed – see SLICE.

POACH: to cook in liquid on the fire or in the oven.

PURÉE: fruit or vegetables after sieving.

QUATRE-ÉPICES: a mixture of spices, sold in France under this name.

REDUCE: to cook in order to evaporate water and thicken the remaining sauce (i.e. reduce its bulk).

ROUX: flour and butter cooked together; a white *roux* is colourless; a medium *roux*, cooked more, is pale brown; a brown *roux*, cooked longer, is brown.

SAUTER: to cook dry material in a fairly small amount of fat on the top of the fire – as distinct from frying which involves the use of more fat and cooking faster.

SEASON: to add salt, pepper, etc.

SHRED: to cut in long, thin slices.

SIMMER: to cook just at boiling point.

SIPPETS: the old English word for *croûtons*.

SLICE OF LEMON: a thin piece of lemon, cut latitudinally from the fruit and used mainly for decoration (see PIECE OF LEMON).

VELOUTÉ: white *roux* to which veal- or chicken-stock or fish-stock has been added.

ZEST (French, ZESTE): the outer, shiny skin of an orange or lemon.

Equivalent Measures

A standard English measuring-cup holds 10 liquid ounces – that is,
½ pt (Imperial measure), whereas an American measuring cup holds
8 liquid ounces, an American ½ pt. When dry ingredients are meas-
ured in a cup their weight (avoirdupois) will obviously vary with
their density. A table showing some equivalent measures in American
cups is given below.

    1 lb. flour (16 oz. avoirdupois)   = 4 cups sifted flour
    ½ lb. granulated and caster sugar = 1 cup
    ½ lb. brown sugar   = 1¼ cups
    ½ lb. butter   = 1 cup

When spoon measurements are given, the spoons are rounded,
that is, they have as much above the bowl of the spoon as below.

Oven Temperatures

	Degrees Fahrenheit	Regulo (for gas cookers)	Degrees Centigrade
Very slow	240–80	$\frac{1}{4}$–$\frac{1}{2}$	115–35
Slow	280–320	1	135–60
Warm	320–40	3	160–70
Moderate	340–70	4	170–85
Fairly hot	370–400	5–6	185–205
Hot	400–40	7	205–25
Very hot	440–80	8–9	225–50

Index

Index